Garlic Is Life

A Memoir with Recipes

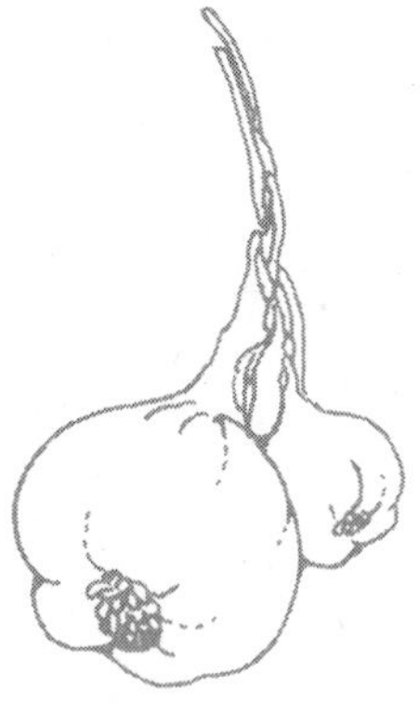

CHESTER AARON

Ten Speed Press
Berkeley, California

Ten Speed Press
Post Office Box 7123
Berkeley, California 94707

Distributed in Australia by E. J. Dwyer Pty. Ltd., in Canada by Publishers Group West, in New Zealand by Tandem Press, in South Africa by Real Books, and in the United Kingdom and Europe by Airlift Books.

Cover design Nancy Austin
Interior design by Catherine Jacobes
First five photographs by Paul Bloom, all others by Robert Kourik

Library of Congress Cataloging-in-Publication Data
Aaron, Chester, 1923–
Garlic is life / Chester Aaron
p. cm.
ISBN 0-898-15-806-0
1. Aaron, Chester, 1923– . 2. Garlic growers--California--Biography.
3. Garlic--California. 4. Farm life--California.
I. Title.
SB63.A18A3 1996
635' .26--dc20
[B] 95-40815
CIP

First printing, 1996
Printed in Canada

1 2 3 4 5 - 00 99 98 97 96

For Louis Segal

Since I met you when you were...what...three years old,
you've been (for the last forty-two years) in my mind
with such force that you are now in my blood. You are not
my stepson anymore, you are a much admired
and much-beloved son.

Contents

A Statement on Taste

by Ron Engeland

From a Filaree Farm catalog
Okanogan, Washington

NO TWO PEOPLE DESCRIBE GARLIC the same, even when tasting the exact same clove. Garlic taste varies depending on soil, weather, culture, and length of storage.

Garlic taste is complex. It includes not only a flavor, but aroma and texture. It's strongly affected by "reflex taste," which is not a true taste but a reaction to hotness or burning. Finally, many garlics have an aftertaste.

All these factors are variable in and of themselves; for instance, some garlics are hotter than others, but cold winters can make them even hotter. In general, any kind of stress, such as extreme cold or sudden extreme heat, can enhance the red colors in garlic, and there is often some corelation between the amount of red and the amount of heat. There are also different kinds of heat—some explode in your mouth and then dissipate, some are fiery and burning, others build slowly in warmth without reaching unpleasant levels.

A really great raw garlic has the right balance of heat and flavor. Both should be enjoyable. Texture should not be grainy or greasy, and aftertaste must not be metallic or burning.

Of course, most Americans don't eat raw garlic at all. They prefer cooked or powdered garlic. Some strains taste bland as raw garlic but rate highly when cooked or roasted. A grainy textured garlic might make great pesto.

We've included a few comments on raw taste for some of the strains in this catalogue, but we urge you not to take them as gospel. Remember also that many garlics require a year or two of "settling in" to a new soil and climate.

We will, however, offer you our own biased personal opinions about general varietal tastes. We think Rocamboles are the best flavored raw garlics, and they don't lose much when cooked. Artichoke strains can nearly equal Rocamboles only when grown in ideal environments. Furthermore, Artichokes tend to deteriorate in quality when cooked.

Porcelain and Purple Stripe garlics are similar to Rocamboles but tend to have more zip. Like Rocamboles, they seem to retain most of their quality when cooked. Silverskins can taste good raw when grown in ideal environments, but in many locations they're the blandest or the hottest tasting garlics. On the other hand, they seem to gain character and flavor when cooked, sometimes outscoring Rocamboles.

Bear in mind that the foregoing statements are broad generalities. There will always be exceptional strains that rise above the rest, and each new harvest will include its varied and subtle nuances. Remember also that taste alone doesn't make the garlic. Length of storage can be an important factor, as can "workability" in the kitchen, or just plain productivity in the garden. Each varietal type has its strong and weak points and each deserves a place in our cuisine.

Acknowledgments

Sherry Arden, new agent, new friend, who fed me hope.

Ron Engeland, farmer and author, whose research and recommendations have been my guide. I am also grateful to him for allowing me to quote from his previously published descriptions of many garlic species.

Donald Fanger, old friend, professor, linguist, author, critic, whose suggestions were tough and astute and whose knowledge of the Russian language saved me.

Faye Mulligan, tough, bright, indulgent teenage worker who stayed with me in the hot sun and cold mud—planting, weeding, watering, mulching—and all for far lower wages than she deserved.

Robert Kourik, friend, grower, author, whose wit kept me laughing and whose genius goes virtually unrecognized, and without whose help and advice I'd be harvesting dust.

For Spanish translation, I am grateful to Annie Neustadter.

CHAPTER 1

Garlic, Gophers, and Sadie

GOPHERS LOVE TO EAT GARLIC. Sadie, my cat, loves to eat gophers.

Over the seven years that Sadie has owned me she has caught approximately two thousand gophers. This morning, a few minutes after sunrise, she caught the czar—or perhaps the czarina—of all gophers.

I awoke when the alarm sounded at six and went downstairs. Not expecting to have to go outside, I wore no slippers.

I turned on the lights that line the path reaching from my garlic-curing shed to my front deck, and I opened and closed the door, but Sadie did not appear.

Summer or winter, on those nights when she chooses to stay outside, Sadie comes galloping down the path or along the side deck the moment the door opens or the lights go on. If she doesn't appear right away, a few taps of a knife on the edge of her kibble bowl is a signal she can't resist.

But this morning my taps on the bowl were unsuccessful.

Even though I was barefoot, I decided to go outside. I was sure I'd find Sadie stretched out on the railing, her favorite observation site. From there, day or night, she can study the sloping meadow and keep watch on my forty garlic boxes.

Sadie is familiar with the distinct personality of each of these boxes. There are seven or eight—the older boxes—that are the targets of particularly persistent gophers forever probing the wire floors. The rusting wire on these older boxes promises them, eventually, luscious garlic.

They know that the fine mesh wire on the newer boxes denies them entry for another five or six years. But they are there, I know. As does Sadie. Their miniature volcano mounds surround the boxes like bogs of quicksand. One misstep and your foot disappears.

Day and night, except during winter storms, Sadie patrols those old boxes, a dedicated soldier prepared for battle with a ruthless foe.

While I waited at the railing, the sunlight intensified and I finally saw Sadie below me, at the front edge of box No. 4, concentrating on a patch of grass at her front feet. My own feet were freezing and I needed my coffee, but I was reluctant to distract her.

As she continued to stare at the patch of grass at her front left foot, she slowly, silently, arched her back. Her haunches, quivering, readied her body for the spring. So gradually as to be almost imperceptible, her right foot rose almost to her ear.

The strike of the right claw was sudden, swift, and successful. I saw what appeared to be a squirrel flying through the air.

Sadie leaped, twisting her body in mid-flight to catch the squirrel between her front claws. Growling, screeching, the two of them rolled about on the grass in what seemed to be deadly combat.

I feared for Sadie. Squirrels can be devastating to cats. But Sadie, on her back in the high weeds, was now hugging the enemy to her chest and clawing its belly.

No more ferocious sound has ever spilled out of Sadie's throat.

Then, ripping free of Sadie's claws, the squirrel raced across the grass and passed through a patch of clear sunlight—revealing itself to be not a squirrel but a gopher. Probably the largest gopher that has ever lived.

If that giant gopher had survived and had succeeded in breaking into one of my boxes, it could have pulled every stalk of garlic down into its burrow in an hour.

But it did not survive. Now the beast was running for its life, searching for a hole. Sadie, still screaming, pounced on the gopher's back. It stretched out, lay still, and its soul ascended to gopher heaven.

A week ago, at around three in the morning, I awoke from a nightmare. Sadie, sitting on the rim of box No. 5 (which contains my two mystery garlics, as well as fifty stalks of Polish Carpathian Red), was playing Mozart's Concerto No. 4 in D Major on Isaac Stern's Stradivarius. The melody is not a tribute to joy.

Gophers.

If just one gopher breaks through the wire on one of the boxes, it could wipe out a substantial fraction of what fractional profit I might have earned this year.

Sadie is an ocelot of cat.

I'm not sure whether I was rebelling against my father or cheering my mother when, about seven years ago, just about the time I started planting my exotic garlics, I yielded to Sadie's charms and permitted her to adopt me.

What, you ask, does Sadie have to do with garlic?

Well, as you know now, Sadie kills gophers—those cute, cuddly, toothy little beasts that inhabit children's stories.

In the wild, at least in *my* wild, gophers destroy dreams.

From my first season in Occidental to now, today, this minute, I have tried *everything* I and others could think of to eliminate the little pests. And I have failed.

Traps: too cruel. So-called gopher plants: ineffectual and ugly. Arsenic: possibly dangerous to people, pets, and birds if not handled correctly. Whirligig propellers stuck in the ground: silly eyesores that only drive the miniature monsters to another tunnel ten yards away. Gas bombs: expensive, foul smelling, ineffectual, and reminiscent of the holocaust.

I have to admit that, driven to an uncontrollable rage the third year I lived here, when gophers took down half of my corn seedlings, several of my tomato plants, and almost all of Dominic Albini's precious white-skinned garlic, I spent hours and many dollars on so-called remedies. Nothing worked. The gophers only multiplied. In desperation, on the advice of a neighbor, I used about twenty gallons of gas to pipe fumes from my car's exhaust pipe into the gopher runs. The gophers must have had gas masks tucked away, because they not only survived, they multiplied.

I calculated that each of the ten moderately sweet and severely disfigured tomatoes I harvested that year cost me roughly eight dollars. From thirty defeated and demeaned stalks of Silver Queen corn, I harvested a total of seven ears that tasted like dry corn flakes. Each ear cost me at least four dollars.

Five or six years ago, using six traps, I'd had what I'd considered a fairly successful gopher season. In a gopher-skin cap, I would have been a stocky, elderly GeorgianJewishDavyCrockett.

Near the end of that summer, the neighbor who'd advised me to gas my gophers dropped by again. He appraised the hundreds of mounds surrounding my garlic boxes.

He tilted his cowboy hat lower over his eyebrows and shook his head in commiseration. "You got yourself a passel of gophers," he said.

I had to demonstrate that I was not just off the turnip truck. "I'm getting them, Bert. Killed 119 so far this summer."

He nodded. The hat fell lower over his eyes. He studied the field another minute and spit again. "How many acres?"

"Five."

"Five acres, 119 gophers." He nodded, thought again, spit again. "Haven't touched 'em."

A local paper recently ran a story about a stained diary found in the attic of an old home in Sebastopol, about ten miles from my home in Occidental. The diary contains entries written by one of the Russian soldiers who had traveled south from Alaska in the 1830s. He may have been one of the troopers in the contingent that built Fort Ross on the coast, sixty miles north of Occidental. One translated excerpt from the diary was of great interest to me: "...we could have survived on this land if it weren't for the ground rats..."

As Sadie marched in victory around the corpse of the monster gopher, I went into the house to build a fire in the iron stove. I made coffee and spread a plate with four of my favorite foods: two slices of toasted Pugliese bread covered with butter and blackberry jam (made by Nancy, a friend in Berkeley, who'd picked six quarts of my berries last summer), and two slices of bruschetta, light toast rubbed on both sides with fresh garlic, daubed with extra-virgin olive oil, salted and peppered. Breakfast on the deck, one of my most intense pleasures, was about to happen.

The sun, reaching the far grove of redwoods, had opened what had been a single black mass into a collection of majestic trees, several of them two to three hundred feet tall and five to six feet in diameter. Any meal on the deck, in any season, at any hour of the day, is, for me, like dining in the company of monarchs. The redwoods rise out of the earth with dark nobility.

The morning and evening breezes, coming from the west and slipping over the hills and across the flat meadows below, carry the scent of ocean.

When I stepped through the front door, bones crunched under my right foot and, I am convinced, I heard squeals.

Sadie had placed the remains of her trophy on my door mat, precisely where my naked right foot landed.

A forgiving man, I simply prepared a second breakfast.

My father loved garlic but hated cats. My very proper but fiercely independent mother, throughout her married life, carried on a secret extramarital affair with cats.

Sometimes, I hear my mother's cool and elegantly modulated voice subduing my father's tempestuous cries of outrage at my having wasted so much time working in Berkeley, then so much time on the sheep ranch in Bodega, then so much time here, in Occidental, planting, as he would call it, "That *fershtunkena* white garlic. Pi-tooey!"

How many times, as a child and as an adolescent, had I witnessed my father's disagreement with a number of actions that he evidently considered crimes: his bushy brows lowered, his eyes almost closed, his mouth puckered as if preparing to spit out the ultimate all-inclusive curse: *"Pi-tooey!"*

I see that boulder of a man behind my childhood house, pulling out of the soil a handful of long green leaves with, at the end, an object as large as his fist. I see him squatting there, the red-black root extended and shaken to clear it of soil. The explosion of sharp garlic pungency that invades the air settled in my ragged sweater and shirt, in my long winter underwear. Wherever I wandered, in the classroom, on the playground, or, at night, huddled beneath the blankets, I tasted garlic at the back of my throat.

Now, on the deck, considering the coming day's work in the fields, I see myself, that twelve- or thirteen-year-old boy, kneeling next to my father who—if I had only known—would be dead in seven years.

I know now, without his ever having told me, that as a boy *he* had knelt in a Georgian field in just such reverential awe at the side of *his* father. He too had huddled beneath the blankets in the cold Tochliavari darkness, remembering *his* father's fist filled with the dark red root and tasting, at the back of *his* thirteen-year-old throat, the rich rush of garlic.

History is genetic.

We don't know for certain where the wild progenitor of garlic originated. Botanists' varying claims include: the mountains of Central Asia, the high plains of West-Central Asia, and the Kirgiz desert of Western Russia.

At any rate, the plant, perhaps carried and spread by nomadic tribes, was known to be cultivated in the Middle East at least five thousand years ago, perhaps more.

Evidence of its use predates the pharaohs. There are clay models of the head that have been dated back to 3750 B.C.

Garlic was used in Egypt for food, medicine, and religious ceremonies. On record is the use of garlic by the slaves who built Khufu's great pyramid at Gizeh, and the herb was found in the tomb of King Tutankhamen, as well as in other less-famous tombs.

The Talmud, the ancient Jewish book of law and tradition, tells us that married couples should eat garlic on Friday night, the Sabbath, so that, in the biblical sense, they might know each other better.

Aristotle recommended garlic as a tonic, and Pliny the Elder taught that when pounded with fresh coriander and drunk with wine, garlic acts as an aphrodisiac. (I tried this on the eve of my seventy-first birthday.) Pliny also claimed that garlic is an antidote against the poison of various animals and plants. I've not needed to test this yet.

The first part of the oldest Sanskrit manuscript in existence is devoted entirely to garlic, describing Indian medical traditions dating back to the sixth century B.C.

Roman legions used garlic to improve their health. They also planted garlic with roses and violets around their forts and villas, and were responsible for introducing the bulb to Britain. The word *garlic* originates from the Anglo-Saxon *gar-leac*, or "spear-plant."

Allium, the Latin name for garlic, is derived from the Celtic *all,* signifying hot or burning.

Sativum means planted, cultivated, or sown (not wild). The genus includes as many as seven hundred species.

An ancient herbalist named Dioscorides identified one variety of the plant as "serpent garlic" because of its coiling flower stalks. In Greek, snake equals ophis. Thus: *Ophioscorodon,* known in my boxes as rocambole, or serpent hardneck garlic.

The *Kyranides*, a Greek collection of remedies from the Roman Empire, advises readers who fear the presence of snakes to "eat garlic ahead of time and drink hot blood with wine." I've always liked my blood at body temperature, however.

The use of garlic was widespread during the Great Plague of 1665 and, afterward, in many cholera epidemics. Today, medical newsletters from prestigious medical schools all over the country report the financing of research programs that result in praising the virtues of garlic in the treatment of practically every disease that affects the body—from the outer perimeter of the cranium to the epidermis of the sole of the foot. Some of the claims are undoubtedly stretching the truth, but others (such as garlic lowering blood pressure) just might be true.

For much of the above information, I am indebted to Rosemary Titterington and Steven Foster, who whose articles in *The Garden* and the American Botanical Council's *Botanical Series* caught my eye.

OK. A small serving of pseudo-scientific jargon.

Get ready. This is a test.

Garlic is *Allium sativum.*

Isn't the onion also an *Allium* ?

Genetically and visibly, *Allium sativum* is distinguished from *Allium fistulosim* (the bunching onion) or from *Allium cepa* (the common red-purple or common yellow-brown or common white) onions, and from other *Allium cepa* (*Aggregatim* group) such as potato onions or purple topsets or shallots (at last count approximately seventy-seven varieties), and from *Allium ampeloprasum* (the onion leek).

Not all *Alliums* are created equal.

Go bite into a clove of the garlic on the shelves or in the bins of almost any supermarket in any city in the United States. Whether shipped from Oregon or Mexico or California (and now China), it will almost certainly be the white-skinned variety commonly called California Early or California Late. That is the garlic 98 percent of the world's current consumers know as *garlic*.

White garlic. As in *white-skinned*. Very hot white-skinned.

A squat white turban of white garlic ranges in weight from two ounces to six or eight ounces. The current price in the local market bins, as of this minute: $2.59 a pound. Depending on when you buy it and where it comes from, it will survive on your shelf for about a month before it begins to deteriorate (meaning to shrink, to lose strength, to shoot up a green tip, to soften, and eventually to smell rotten).

In their elegies to garlic, could Aristotle and Hippocrates and Pliny the Elder have possibly been referring to this white California garlic that throws a bite so intense that it numbs lips and palate, destroying the flavor of the garlic itself?

Not likely.

After I harvest this coming summer, in three or four months, I will have lines of bundled garlics hanging in my curing shed. Some heads will be small, some large; some will be shaped like the "ordinary" garlic (the classic "turban"), some will look like artichokes or cacti or carbuncles, and some like the onion domes of Russian Orthodox churches. A few will send long white banners from the tips of their cloves.

These were undoubtedly the garlics so admired by those ancients. No California White garlic for Herodotus, the Greek historian and "Father of History," who informs us that there is an inscription of Egyptian characters on a pyramid that records the quantities of radishes, onions, and garlic consumed by the laborers who built the monstrous honorific.

Extraordinary humans, those immortal Greek mortals. Nothing ordinary for them. They relied, I am certain, on *extraordinary* garlic.

They would have gone bonkers over my Russian Red Toch.

When my own supply of Russian Red Toch—one variety of the thirty (thirty-two?) garlics I now grow in my forty boxes—dwindles and I am fortunate enough to find a grower (or a visitor from the Republic of Georgia) who can spare me ten or fifteen heads, the garlic costs me $28.00 a pound. What do I sell it for? $5.50 a pound.

So I lose $22.50 for each pound I sell?

Oh yes, I am my father's son.

Back to my Russian Red Toch.

Like my other thirty (thirty-two?) varieties of garlic, Russian Red Toch is certainly not white. Nor is it ordinary.

My Russian Red Toch is a variety of garlic called Artichoke, which belongs to the subspecies *sativum*. The *sativum* is considered a softneck garlic. Softneck garlics—having tops (or greens, or green leaves) that are pliable and easy to braid—are believed to have evolved from the subspecies called *Ophioscorodon*. They've lost the ability to bolt and produce flower stalks with topset bulbils, which are tiny seeds enclosed in a sheath.

To compensate for this loss, softneck garlics generally produce larger bulbs (or heads) with more cloves per head, more fertile leaves, and therefore more clove layers.

Softneck garlics are easier to grow and are more productive per acre. They require less labor and adapt more easily to different soils and climates. They can be very mild or very hot, often lacking the somewhat wild flavor of *Ophioscorodon* garlics. The most widely grown garlics in the world, softnecks can store well on the shelf—as long as six months to a year. When grown well, they can almost equal rocambole (*hardneck*) garlics in flavor.

Both subspecies (*sativum*, or softneck garlics and *ophioscorodon*, or hardneck garlics) belong to the domesticated species called *Allium sativum*.

Species, subspecies, variety, sub-variety: classifications important to biologists, horticulturists, pathologists. Don't worry about them. I don't. I just pretend to be interested.

Here in Occidental I grow mainly rocambole garlics—partly by accident, partly by choice.

Scapes, or seed stalks, which are unique to rocambole garlics, shoot up at the center of the green leaves about four to five months after planting. They coil tightly shortly after they appear, then, perhaps a week later, coil again. The scapes lose all coils within a few weeks and stand up straight. By this time they have turned woody.

Other *Ophio* strains (*strains*: a new term—forget it!) have scapes that form random coils or broad sweeping curls, and some that form arches rather than coils. Ignored, these scapes will produce seed heads at the top, and those heads will open to show colorful blue purple bulbils that are used in some countries in stir-fries or in salads. Replanted, these bulbils may produce thin greens that can be added to salads. Replanted each year for three or four years, the bulbils *might* produce fairly substantial heads.

The single clove from a whole head of rocambole garlic is usually flat at the base. The tip of the clove, usually blunt, can vary in shape from plump and round to narrow and wedge shaped (when planted too early or grown in southern climates). Most rocambole strains average six to eleven cloves to the head.

Do I sound like a professional horticulturist?

Frankly, technical jargon bores me. I'm not filled with scorn, as my father was (especially when my eldest brother, a botanist, spoke the language of the academic theorist), I'm just not interested in that part of the process. Hurrah for those who are. Hurrah, again, for those who prefer Gilroy's white garlics. I myself use them whenever the supply of my own garlic is depleted.

The biological history that defines the neat little adjustments by which the original wild garlics altered their shape and size and color in order to survive does not interest me. I'm merely impressed that garlic exists.

I'm pleased that I can duplicate my choice garlics with my own hands, in my own soil, without ever entering a laboratory to play with DNA or microscopes or test tubes.

But the truth is, when I offer one of the peaches from a tree I planted as a bare root six years ago and I say "This is a Red Haven" or "This is a Babcock" or "This is a Strawberry Nectar," I have to admit I do enjoy the authority my guests grant me. I'm just waiting for some Ph.D. candidate to tell me, "This is not a Red Haven, sir. This is an O'Henry."

People who know less than I do will frequently ask me about the details of horticulture or botany or plant pathology, and my refusal to pretend, my need to say "I don't know," offends them, or supports their belief that farmers are hicks who happen to be lucky. Like most farmers, I have learned in the field, not in the classroom. Today, here in California, as in Iowa, Washington, and Mississippi, the sons and daughters of farmers are getting college degrees in agriculture and business. Farming is not just business these days, it's big business. And big business is big money.

Small farming is small money. Often no money. I am identified as a small farmer in my tax reports. I get certain, very limited, tax breaks that help finance a couple tons of soil or extra sticks of redwood for my next few boxes.

Small farmer. Almost by definition a loser.

Hello, Poppa.

Many years ago, in *Esquire* magazine, Bernard Wolf, a writer and cigar lover, described a visit to Cuba before the revolution destroyed the tobacco industry. A taxi driver berated him for buying green cigars. "Green—*candela*—cigars are for export, *señor*, to America." The driver took Wolf to a *finca*, where Wolf received a gift from the planter's private stock: a *maduro,* not dark brown but black. The cigar oozed oil when squeezed. That was the cigar of Wolf's life.

What are the garlics of my life?

Of my thirty (thirty-two?) children, how dare I say I love one more than another? If tortured, I'd confess. Treated kindly, I'd confess. Without your even asking me, I'll confess.

Number one, of course: Russian Red Toch, which is a pale rose color. To quote Ron Engeland at Filaree Farm on the quality of Russian Red Toch: "Raw taste described as perfect garlic flavor."

Number two, after Russian Red Toch? Several, all relatively unequal in their qualities: Creole Red from Louisiana and Mexico; Spanish Roja; Inchelium Red, reputedly the oldest garlic in North America, discovered on an Indian reservation in the state of Washington; Acropolis, from Greece; Skuri (purple striped, with a mild and earthy raw flavor, from the Republic of Georgia); Yugoslavian (large bulbs, copper veined, purple blotched, and vigorous, with a strong aroma and a hot and spicy taste at first, then a warm, sweet aftertaste); Persian Star (originally from a bazaar in Samarkand, Uzbekistan, with red-tipped cloves and a pleasantly mild taste with a zing of spice); Romanian Red (a Porcelain variety, in my soil purple blotched like some rocamboles, four to five cloves to a head, hot and pungent, with a healthy long-lasting bite and a rich taste after the bite fades); and Metechi (origin unknown, possibly Mexico or even Germany, with few and quite large cloves, and thick, blushed skins; long storing, very fiery when eaten raw but with a nice smooth finish; great for salsa).

And how can I possibly relegate to minority status the Republic of Georgia's La Panant Kari and Poland's Carpathian Red and Korea's Asian Tempest (with a mild, flavorful taste when eaten raw)?

The two parenthetical garlics, for now, are my mystery garlics because their histories and behavior are almost too bizarre for anyone but an obsessed and certified garlic freak to believe. I need to wait until next year's harvest to see if they survive. They've been threatening suicide for two years. To a fundamentalist garlicphile, *suicide* is a sin.

I'm struggling to midwife these two incipient sinners into a rebirth. Over the last two years, most of the cloves of both garlics have died. I all but nursed the survivors at my breast. From what I can see so far, going into their third year, however, there is reason to hope.

—

Back to Sadie.

It has been raining for two days. The ground is soaked. The gophers are rising to the surface because their burrows are being flooded. The rain is not yet heavy enough to deter hawks and owls from circling the fields early morning and late evening, gorging on the victims. A pleasure to behold.

Inside, reduced to using undignified litter boxes because she refuses to get her delicate paws muddy, Sadie observes the raptors with what appears to me to be a mixture of scorn and resentment. She sits on a bolster near the window, her confederate-gray hair backlit by the setting sun.

When one of the great birds plunges, strikes, and rises with a gopher in its claws, Sadie's mouth twitches. Her whiskers tremble.

I stroke her head and murmur sweet nothings to her. I remind her of the saying, "The enemy of my enemy is my friend."

Mary Catherine O'Connor would be jealous if she didn't love cats. "I think I'm going to grow more gray hair," she says. "Just in case. Maybe even develop a taste for gophers."

—

To the true garlicphile, garlic is not just to be eaten, not even just to be tasted. It is to be *savored*.

And oh, I do savor garlic. Both garlic and life.

In fact, garlic is my life.

Why do you think that I, at the age of seventy-two, can still run the hundred-yard dash in under ten seconds? I can't, but why do you think I can?

Aristotle was right. Garlic is a tonic. My special garlics, starting with Russian Red Toch, are special tonics.

Sometimes, those evenings when I sit on the deck with Sadie (her eyes like large amber lozenges), or with my son Louis and his family, or with Mary Catherine, I sip a gin and tonic and remind myself that at the age of seventy-two, I am living an ideal life.

Mary Catherine insists that God, chewing peyote or magic mushrooms or garlic, has, in Her psychedelic ecstasy, reversed the digits.

CHAPTER 2

California Early, California Late

THE TOWN OF BODEGA is seventy miles north of San Francisco and five minutes inland from the Pacific coast.

In the spring, the fog lifts from the surface of the ocean at dusk and rolls eastward to hover over the green fields and the scattered herds of sheep and cattle. Then, as if sucking strength from the approaching darkness, the fog climbs the coastal hills to drift farther eastward, where, until sunrise, it settles over Duncan's Mills and Monte Rio and northern Santa Rosa.

On those infrequent evenings when the fog fails to materialize, nature, abhorring a vacuum, supplies a pattern of winds so cold that stray cattle seek each other out until ten or twenty or thirty, bunched together, find comfort inside their accumulated warmth. Only the smug, snug, thickly coated sheep need not seek shelter behind a barn or outcroppings of huge rocks or within the sheltering groves of oaks or firs or redwood trees.

Locals always have a sweater or jacket available should they be outside after five or six o'clock.

In April, as soon as the ground is willing to accept a spade, the ranchers around Bodega who want summer and autumn vegetables for their kitchens pull on their boots and take down their spades, or attach the rototiller blades to their tractors. They must dig deep to lift and flip the soil until there is a uniform blanket of loose loam, which rarely needs even to be leveled before receiving seeds or seedlings.

In the country around Bodega, as around Occidental—in fact around just about every town in Sonoma County—Italian names prevail: The Orsi cattle ranch, the Petrini dairy, the Gonella Restaurant, the Negri racing stables, Panizzera's Market, Frati and Fiori and Morelli Lanes, Donatelli Plumbing and Lunardi Electric and Calvi Construction.

The first Italians migrated to this part of Northern California during the mid-to-late nineteenth century, and continued arriving well into the early twentieth. They were usually peasants who settled first in San Francisco, then, when the city reached its saturation point for Italians, traveled or were sent farther north to the forests and fields, where they sought out established friends or relatives from their villages in the old country.

In Sonoma County, thousands worked in the lumber, mining, and railroad industries. Their hoarded earnings eventually went into the purchase of land, which then was put to use as cattle or dairy ranches or vineyards.

Dominic Albini owns the sheep ranch in Bodega where I lived for ten years.

Dominic and his family live and work not in Bodega but on a second ranch, twenty minutes south of Bodega, at the edge of a coastal town called Valley Ford.

Dominic's grandparents, in 1848, began on the Bodega ranch what remains an unbroken tradition. In the fenced allotment of soil behind the gray barn—usually around the middle of May—the Albinis plant a variety of tomatoes, peppers, corn, carrots, and basil.

In October, before the ground becomes hardened by winter frost, they plant a separate crop: garlic. In June, when the garden vegetables are beginning to show promise, the garlic is just about ready for harvest.

Dominic gets his garlic from a cousin who, on a two-thousand-acre ranch near Gilroy, produces every year thousands of tons of white-skinned garlic known as California Early or California Late.

The Albinis drive to their relatives' ranch in Gilroy in early September. The two families exchange their various foods and wines, share their stories about births and deaths, marriages, and successes and failures with crops and animals. Then, after supper, Dominic drives the station wagon back to Bodega, his wife and family retelling the stories of the day.

In the well behind the back seat of the station wagon are two mesh bags, each filled with twenty-five pounds of white garlic. Some heads will be used for cooking over the next several months, but most will be stored until October, when the white heads will be separated into cloves and the cloves will be planted in a fragment of that fenced and carefully nurtured space behind the barn.

Twice a year the garden's soil, covered with sheep and cattle manure, supplemented with cuttings of new green weeds, is turned over, usually by Marty, Dominic's son, who brings in one of their smaller tractors. After almost a century of such attention the soil is so rich that, Dominic boasts, even the stones are growing bigger.

Few of the Albini children speak Italian but they all say *basilico*, not *basil*. They do not say *aglio*, they say *garlic*.

The image that the word *garlic* conveys to all of them is the image that came to their ancestors and comes now to shoppers and cooks all over the world: that turban-shaped root with white skin that adds both heat and flavor to all food except, perhaps, apple pie.

The garlic my father grew in western Pennsylvania, near a town called Butler, was never white. When pulled from the ground it appeared to be black. Its sooty, almost unhealthy appearance, I was sure, was simply a result of having nested in coal-befouled mud all winter and spring.

After being hung in the shade to dry and brought into the kitchen and freed of their outer skins, the exposed large heads, it seemed to me, must have been dipped in red paint by a vandal.

For half a century, as I consumed our usual white-skinned garlics, I, like millions of others, praised or criticized the—what shall we call it—the herb, the vegetable, the food.

Why did I wait almost fifty years, a half of one entire century, before I permitted myself—on the Albini sheep ranch in Bodega, California, on a cool day in mid-May in 1976—to remember my father's garlic, to recall, as if it were yesterday, my father bending over his garden, pulling the greens, liberating the root, and sending the aroma of garlic into the warm summer air?

I moved from Berkeley to the Bodega ranch in April, 1976, suffering from lingering pains caused by a divorce a year earlier. Continuing to live in

Berkeley, continuing to see old friends and remember the good days now lost, I admitted only to myself that I just might be going crazy. The memory of my father, out of his mind after my mother died, ending up in the County Poor Farm, was not especially comforting.

The isolation of the ranch threatened at first to intensify my pain, but the sheer physical effort required by my duties as a novice sheepherder gave me little time to practice self-pity. During the cold nights of winter, the time and energy expended on chopping firewood was welcome distraction but it was usually born of severe discomfort.

Daily, hourly, I was too exhausted to luxuriate in self-pity. After all, I was still teaching full time. On Tuesday and Thursday morning, and too often on Wednesday, I drove south to Saint Mary's College for two hours. And two hours north each evening, with bumper-to-bumper traffic each way.

For an 8:20 class I had to leave the ranch house at five, before dawn. Seventeen hours later, I stumbled up the stairs of the ranch house to bed. On the days I was not at the ranch, Dominic or one of his kids carried out my chores. This awkward arrangement, a blessing for me, would eventually be beneficial to the Albinis. After teaching that one month, I would be living in the previously deserted ranch house full time.

I'd taught literature and writing at Saint Mary's College for more than fifteen years. In that time I'd published three short stories and one novel. The rank and tenure committee agreed with my contention that I ought to have the opportunity to try to write a second novel.

I'd not confessed that I needed the time as much to preserve my sanity as to write.

By having carefully selected the months to be covered by my sabbatical, I would be free from mid-May of 1975 through August of 1976. Almost sixteen months.

Taking a full year meant I'd have to survive on half salary. Less than half. A quarter. Because I was sharing whatever I earned with my ex-wife.

This arrangement would cover two lambing seasons, the most difficult time for the Albinis, who were raising sheep on both their Bodega and Valley Ford ranches. A working day for Dominic and his wife and kids meant forty-eight hours. Given my youth and my vast ranch experience, my presence might reduce that to forty-nine.

When I moved onto the Bodega ranch in late April, Dominic and I had agreed on a formula. Until the semester ended I was to pay him one hundred dollars a month. Once I was on the ranch full time, I'd pay forty dollars because I'd be performing duties that were, in Dominic's eyes, worth far more than whatever rent I might pay.

In the remaining bit of spring and the following year, I was responsible for the minor chores that kept the sheep ranch functioning.

My primary duty was to be on the watch for stray dogs. Two dogs could destroy twenty sheep in an hour. Four dogs a hundred sheep, and during lambing season, even more.

I also had to be aware of signs of smoke in the hills or the smell of burning grass. The Bodega Volunteer Fire Department was first rate, but if a major fire swept over the hills, driven by a west or north wind, it could destroy the ranch house and the animals ten minutes after the flames were visible.

Two or three times every day I had to check the iron tubs scattered across the land to be sure the well had filled them with water for the sheep.

Whenever Dominic and the kids came to the ranch to work the sheep, I might be needed to help as best I could, which often meant I contributed far less than their border collies.

During the lambing season—December through February—I walked the hills every morning to evaluate the condition of the ewes and of the lambs born during the night. Dominic had loaned me a pair of binoculars with which to locate any ewes dragging their partially expelled lambs behind them. I carried deserted lambs to the stalls in the barn, where I fed them, using a baby bottle, with a special milk concoction Dominic had drawn from other birthing ewes. That milk, containing the mother's colostrum, had to be in a lamb's gut a few hours after birth to help it develop immunity to various diseases.

Later in the morning Dominic or one of his kids would go up into the hills in the pickup. I'd get into the bed of the truck with the collies. Whenever we'd spot one of the ewes dragging her lamb we'd run her down and Dominic or Marty or Brenda, in a few minutes, would pull the lamb free. It was almost always dead. Lost or orphaned lambs would be transported to the home ranch at Valley Ford, where, if they were lucky, they might be grafted onto a ewe willing and able to accept a replacement for her own lost lamb or lambs.

Dominic loaned me a rifle. Having served in the infantry in combat I was no stranger to weapons. But I loved dogs. This, I knew, could be a problem.

Dominic advised me that I was to shoot any dog that I discovered on the land and bury it. Ranchers could not afford to take the time to prove to the owner—if the dog was wearing a license and the owner could be found—that his/her dog had been on the land killing sheep. The dog owner would sue, the rancher would have to go to court and possibly hire a lawyer. He'd lose four or five days of work.

It was easier and cheaper, Dominic said, to just shoot the dog and bury it. This from a man who said he loved his collies.

But no matter the bloody carnage I came upon, which I did three times that first spring, once with four lambs torn apart, I could never shoot the dogs. I fired over their heads, scaring them across the hills onto the next ranch where, I knew, the chances were good that they'd be shot by someone else. Dominic laughed at my so-called marksmanship.

In late April, a few days after my arrival at the ranch, Dominic asked me if I wanted Marty to bring the tractor and disc a small patch in the field near the house for my garden. Everyone except me just assumed I'd want a summer garden.

Why not? It was one more soul-saving distraction. And the idea of raising my own vegetables appealed to me. I'd not worked in a garden since I was a kid. But how many tomatoes or peppers or ears of corn could one man eat?

"I'll dig up a little patch for myself," I said, as if gardening were an ongoing experience.

"Well," Dominic informed me, "the ground's ready. You sure you don't want Marty to bring the tractor and disc it for you?"

The words *disc* and *tractor* suggested *acreage*. I had in mind a piece of earth half the size of my kitchen floor.

"Thanks, Dominic. I can do it."

"Plenty of tools in the barn," Dominic said. "I got some tomato plants left over. Other stuff too. Want them?"

"Sure, thanks. What do you have?"

He went down the list. I said I'd like a few tomato plants, a few peppers, and some corn.

"Silver Queen corn," he said. Silver Queen, he assured me, was the best white corn in the world. His father and grandfather had planted Golden Bantam right there where I'd be planting my tomatoes. Too bad Silver Queen had not been available.

"And basilico. What's an Italian garden without basilico?"

"I'm not Italian, Dominic."

"The house is," Dominic said, leaning against one of the porch posts as he must have done a thousand times in his childhood and youth. "The land, too."

Dominic's grandfather had planted his first garden in 1850. In the subsequent 125 years, there had been a garden in the same area every summer. Right there, next to the barn. Dominic's father was ten years old when *his* father built the fence that still keeps out the deer.

This year, Dominic complained, would be the first year since 1850 that no Albini would have a garden on this site.

I suggested that Dominic could adopt me, and I could change my name, but he declined. Maybe he'd take a small patch and plant some basilico. The house would cry if it couldn't have pesto in the kitchen. "We scrubbed the walls," Dominic said, "but 125 years of pesto—well, we couldn't get rid of it. You smell it the minute you open the door."

"I'm adding to the smell, Dominic. I eat a lot of pasta. Pesto's my favorite sauce."

"It is? Okay, then I don't feel too bad."

Dominic promised to bring the plants in two days. Tomatoes, corn, beans, basilico. Tomorrow morning he'd be here early. He and Marty and Brenda. They had to worm the ewes and dock the lambs' tails.

"You see that garlic growing right over there, in that corner? There's fifty stalks. Planted a hundred cloves last October. The gophers got fifty. If we're lucky, around June, we'll have forty, maybe. I'll come over to help you dig it up. Then, next October, we'll start all over again. A hundred more cloves."

"So I'll have three months to eat fifty cloves of garlic?"

"Fifty *heads*. Each clove you plant becomes a whole head."

"That's a lot of garlic, Dominic."

He clapped me on the back. "Hey, your hair's going thin. Garlic will bring it back thick again. Black. Look at my hair."

"Take off your hat, Dominic."

He laughed. "I mean the hair you can see."

"It's gray, Dominic."

"It is? Damn, Chester, you got any garlic in the house? I only had three cloves for breakfast this morning."

I worked with the Albinis and their border collies, chasing the sheep out of the hills and into the holding pens near the barn.

The dogs hustled the sheep through a chute that emptied into a small pen. There they were dipped, one by one, in a trough filled with a copper solution that kills mites and ticks and eases any general infections. Brenda and Suzie, wearing boots and rubber aprons and rubber gloves, worked alongside Marty, Dominic, and me. After each ewe was immobilized, Dominic, with the finesse of an experienced nurse, worked a tube down her throat. Medicine flowed into every stomach, young and old, to rid the animal of parasites and worms. Their backs were daubed with a red dye to indicate they'd been medicated, and they were sent along their way.

Except for the lambs. These suffered the pain of having their long tails cut off with a knife.

The women and I did the holding, Marty and Dominic did the cutting. The knives flashed once over each lamb, and an antibiotic spray soaked each bloody stump. Then, wormed and dipped and daubed red, the lambs rushed into the field to find and be found by their mothers.

It was almost dark when we finished with the last ewe and lamb. We still had to chase the four rams, which was like catching and throwing four speeding steam engines off their tracks and rolling them over by hand while the wheels were still revolving and smoke was still belching from the stacks.

We stood around after the work was completed, drinking beer.

Dominic informed me that he made his own wine, regular Dago red. He'd bring me a bottle. "Think he's man enough, Marty?"

Dominic's son, a tall, broad shouldered, serene teenager, grinned. I'd done pretty well, he said, for someone who'd never worked sheep before. Maybe I could handle the wine.

Dominic warned me that I'd be hearing the sheep bawling all night.

By sunrise everything would be quiet. They will have found each other by then. He assured me that he and Marty could dig up my garden in less than an hour. I thanked him. He had to be as tired as I was. I promised I'd have it ready the next morning.

The next morning I rushed through my breakfast and found a spade and a pick and shovel. The sparse growth of weeds at the site of my future garden was cleared in minutes. I hesitated a moment over the choice of tools. The shovel or the spade? The soil seemed so soft that I chose the shovel. I did not even have to use my foot to drive in the blade. With the first thrust of the shovel, the first lift and flip of the earth, I almost swooned.

There was my father, kneeling at my side, lifting a handful of the upturned earth to his nose.

For a moment, in one of those spasms of confusion that often follows a painful shock, I had the sensation that I was my own father.

Ten years after turning that first shovelful of earth on a sheep ranch in Bodega I would be living in my new home in Occidental, twenty miles to the east, and planting garlic.

But not California White.

CHAPTER 3

A Visit from the King

THE SEMESTER ENDED in late May. I was free.

Most of June and July I worked with the Albinis, picking away at the variety of those ranch jobs that are never mentioned in cowboy movies: checking and repairing fence lines; stacking hay bales in the barn; moving the sheep from a depleted grazing area to another, more lush area; working with the dogs to bring the hundreds of sheep into corrals to be shorn and wormed and dipped in copper sulphate solution to eliminate ticks and foot rot. And finally, culling from their more fortunate relatives (those to be kept alive for one more year, for breeding) the ewes and lambs doomed to be sold, slaughtered, sliced and chopped up, and packaged for the local supermarkets.

Occasionally the Albinis would have me over for supper at their Valley Ford ranch. It was a prized cultural relief to be talking not about campus politics or the relation of faculty tenure to the famine crisis in Eritrea or the significance of the semicolon in Humphrey Humperdink's French translation of the truncated version of Tolstoy's *War and Peace,* but about ranching.

This was a new and romantic world for me. I was not doing it for a living, so I could afford the romantic perception.

Often, after supper, I'd make notes about that day's work at the Bodega ranch and the occasional suppers and discussions at Valley Ford: the return of coyotes to Sonoma County and the potential hazards to sheep (as if the stray dogs roaming the hills were not hazard enough); the declining prices paid for wool and meat, and the improbability of reversing the trend; the questionable benefits of buying and training sheepdogs; and the various options for the recently cleared thirty-acre slope facing the sea: Should we grow oats, potatoes, corn, soybeans, or hold the slope for grazing? Would fog-drip supply enough moisture so that the use of precious water for irrigation might be minimized no matter the crop? Which crop, if any, would, in the end, require the least labor and the most financial rewards?

The discussion of sheepdogs could become quite heated, with stories that proved border collies superior or inferior to Australian shepherds or McNabs, and Dominic's doubts about having dogs at all. There was general agreement that no dog, no matter the breed, would ever repay the original investment, let alone ongoing expenses. Because of an inherited gene, border collies at that time could be vulnerable to blindness before their fifth or sixth year. (This tendency has diminished now, thanks to controlled breeding.) Given the cost of vet bills for the treatment of various other diseases as well as accidents—cuts and bruises from barbed wire and nails and rambunctious rams, infections from foxtails embedded between toes or even death from inhaling them—expensive pups might not be worth the investment by a small rancher.

"Small rancher?" Dominic fumed. "I run darn near a thousand sheep on my two ranches."

"I'll bet," I managed to put in, "if you compute the number of man hours ('And woman hours,' Suzie tossed off)—and woman hours—that are saved, at say five dollars an hour (Suzie: 'Say eight to ten dollars')—say eight to ten dollars—I'll bet the dogs end up saving you money. Time is money. Think about the time they save you."

"And dogs don't have unions to battle," Marty said.

Suzie: And no social security to pay.

Brenda: Or workers' comp.

Me: And they scare off coyotes, don't they?

The kids, as well as Dominic and Mary, tried but failed to restrain their laughter.

"Collies," Dominic said in the tone of a father lovingly correcting an ignorant child, "are not fighters. They'll run from fishin' worms."

Brenda's turn to be outraged. "That's not true, Daddy."

That first summer progressed through periods of pleasant discovery.

Involved in a new way of life that required attention to more physical demands, I found myself thinking less and less about my failed marriage, about my ex-wife, about my contributions to my son's possibly scarred future (scarred by my failure as either husband or father).

I called my son Louis now and then. He was an adult, an adult radical, convinced he knew more about what was good and evil in the world we shared than I did. I rebelled against his rebellions. I listened with patience to his arguments against the Vietnam War, against what he termed "imperialist Israel," in support of the coming revolution in Amer*k*a. (You could hear the *k* though he never spelled it out.) He considered of minimal consequence my own similar experiences thirty years before he'd been born, when I'd wasted (my own judgment, in retrospect) my time, my passion, and my talent on similar holy missions.

I and all my now-fifty-year-old friends had failed, as I was convinced he and his generation would fail.

At the time, I'd longed to take Louis into my arms and plead to him to avoid making the same mistakes I'd made, but, as he and I now know, we all have to make our own mistakes should others fail to make them for us.

Unfortunately, I did not then have the patience or the tact we both have today, in 1996, when I am over seventy and he is over forty, with children of his own—children whose world when they are in their twenties will probably be as alien to him as ours had been to each other.

The fifty California White garlic bulbs Dominic had given me yielded, after my greedy daily consumption, one hundred cloves— enough to plant, and more than enough to satisfy my needs.

In early October, I planted them in a circle about twenty feet in diameter around the outer edge of the rectangular garden that had filled my summer and early fall table with offerings of Beefsteak tomatoes and red and green peppers and basil and six rows (each ten feet long) of Silver Queen corn.

Late in the winter I received three catalogues offering the sale of seeds for rare vegetables: *Southern Exposure Seed Catalogue, Seed Savers Exchange Catalogue,* and *Salt Spring Seed Catalogue* from British Columbia.

My friends say it was fate.

My mother's influence? Possibly, since she often broke traditions.

In late April, in among Dominic's traditional plantings went five varieties of tomatoes (Sweet 100s, Sweet Million, Sun Gold, Husky Red, Great White), two pepper plants (Quadrati d'Asti Giallo, meaning yellow, and Rosso, large, bell shaped, four lobed, deep gold and red, and sweet), and two rows of carrots (one Minicor, from Holland, and one Ingot-hybrid, which carries more than double the amount of carotene than do most other varieties).

Without informing Dominic, I'd followed the recommendations of the catalogues for starting the seeds in potting soil in miniature plastic hothouses inside my home. By the time Dominic planted his seeds, my exotic seedlings were six inches high. And hearty, already prepared for outside weather.

Dominic observed them but never asked me about them. When the offerings came in the autumn, I shared them with the Albinis and they all appreciated the new sights and tastes, especially Brenda. She was passionately devoted to anything, animal or vegetable, that grew in or on the land. I would now and then catch her observing a lamb or a calf or a new fruit tree as if it were a just-discovered brother or sister.

When I had planted the garlic cloves in October, just as the vegetables were disappearing, I'd not planned to form a circle. It just happened. My mother talking?

Near the end of November, when the garlic tips began to push up out of the earth like sharp green dragons' teeth, Dominic strolled over to observe my nearly empty garden.

"Look at the way you planted those garlics. What do you call those guys in the army? You know, they stand guard and blow their trumpets when the enemy shows up?"

"Guards?"

"No, no, no."

"Scouts?"

"Come on, you're a professor. The word makes me think of Central Bank."

"Central. Oh, sentinel?"

"That's it. Sentinels. Your garlics look like sentinels. No bugs or worms gonna get past them without a fight. Who taught you to plant that way? I never planted in circles."

"My father," I said. The response had been immediate.

"Your father planted a garden? In circles? Where? Not in California."

"No, in Pennsylvania. Before that, as a child, in Georgia. He used to work in the garden with his father. His father planted a circle of garlic around his garden."

"Georgia?"

"Russian Georgia."

"Your father planted garlic?"

"He sure did."

"I never heard of a Russian Italian."

"He wasn't a Russian Italian. He was a Russian Georgian Jew."

"Jews eat garlic?"

"That Jew did. And this one."

As we leaned on the fence built by Dominic's grandfather, I thought again of my own father.

But the vision was altered. It was more intense, more immediate. As a result of my time on the Bodega ranch, I had begun to redefine my memories of my childhood. Memories of faces and voices and activities now had sharper edges, fuller bodies.

Now, through the loving eyes of a thirteen-year-old boy, I saw my father (short, stocky, bald) walking around his garden in Pennsylvania; my father (loose black sweater patched at the elbows, dirt-stained pants rolled up above his knotted shoelaces) kneeling down to push a stubby finger into the soil to produce a hole; my father ("I plant for us, this land, this house, our garden, our own garden, boychik!") walking the circle again, this time settling into every moist hole a single garlic clove, flat end down, pointed tip up.

The garlic my father planted, I told Dominic, had red skin. I'd just remembered that. After the dirt had been dried and brushed away and the outside skins removed, the interior skins were rosy red.

Dominic shook his head. Garlic has white skin. What my father planted was probably beets.

He planted beets, I insisted, *inside* the garlic circle. He used to say that garlic fights off bugs and worms. His vegetables always won blue ribbons at the county fair. The biggest this, the best that. He said his special spray helped as much as the garlic.

Special spray? Dominic was intrigued now.

"My father kept a stack of clean flour sacks behind the counter in the store. Every night he poured everything in the spittoons—cigarettes, cigars, chewing tobacco, juices—into a flower sack and squeezed everything through the sack into a big jug. In summer and autumn he sprayed the plants with the stinking stuff once a week. I never saw a single worm."

One evening that summer, after I'd made a pasta with several cloves of garlic Dominic had given me (to hold me over until my own were ready), I called Dominic to tell him I was worried. The leaves on my garlic stalks were going brown. Would the fifty-four garlics have evaded the gophers only to be victims of my incompetence?

The next day, before we toured the hills in his pickup, Dominic stood at the fence and sipped the hot coffee I'd brought him. "Nothing to worry about," he said. "Your garlic's talking to you. 'I'm not going to grow any more, Chester. Dry me off, Chester.' That's what it's telling you. 'Don't water me any more, Chester. In two or three weeks you can dig me up.' That's what it's saying."

Seventy-four garlic stalks, each of them as thick as my thumb, survived that winter of 1976 and spring of 1977. The gophers had taken the other twenty-six. In Valley Ford, Dominic had lost more than half his garlic. "Next fall," he said, "I'm planting in a circle."

Dominic's father had planted garlic twice a year. His cousin down in Gilroy also puts in two cash crops a year.

The two-crop garlic pattern had no appeal for Dominic. His experience with manipulating the cycles of sheep so that they would produce lambs twice a year was equivalent, he was certain, with forcing the land to do more than it should. Ewes that produced twice a year did not live as long as protected ewes. The lambs they produced were not as plump or tasty at the spring auction.

For Dominic the best garlic was planted in October. It had time to set down its roots before cold weather arrived and so would survive the winter better. It would reap more benefits from the hot summer sun. The healthier, stronger heads he grew verified his theories.

"So I ought to pull my garlic?"

I was to hold off from watering for two or three weeks, Dominic said. He'd keep checking it. At Valley Ford, his garlic received more moisture, including fog-drip. It was not yet beginning to brown. He'd tell me when my leaves were brown enough for the stalk to be pulled.

"After you harvest, hang it on the back porch for two weeks. It's shady there and gets the cool breezes."

"Damn, Dominic. I don't know what you'd do if I wasn't here. Who'd you have to give all this advice to? You know more about more things than any of my colleagues at the college."

Dominic grinned and looked away and shuffled his feet. He pretended to think I was teasing him. I think I convinced him I wasn't.

Walking the hills with Dominic one morning during the lambing season I saw, on every telephone pole and fence post, a big California turkey vulture. I considered those vultures the ugliest birds in California. They looked as if they'd eaten too much red meat and it had all stuck in their throats. Wasn't Dominic ever moved to shoot them?

"Chester, they have a job to do. They eat the placenta the ewes leave behind. When a ewe or a lamb goes down, I don't have to bury them. Twenty-four hours, the buzzards got it picked clean to the bones. They do a job for me and for nature."

I tried to wipe my humiliation away with humor. "You like mosquitoes too?"

Dominic, as if explaining the facts of life to an imbecile, reminded me that mosquitoes and moths and other night-flying insects provide food for swallows and bats. Bat dung was just about the best fertilizer a man can get. "If there wasn't mosquitoes, Chester, there wouldn't be bat dung. God didn't create anything without a reason."

Me, the learned professor, the committed ecologist.

In the middle of July, I'd had a call from John Harris, a former housemate and the author of *The Book of Garlic.* "Where the hell did you disappear to, C. A.?"

John sounded just like he had when I'd first met him. "What the hell are you doing in area code 707? Is that Napa?"

"Sonoma."

"What are you doing there? Making wine, I hope?"

"I'm doing odds and ends of work for my room and board."

"You still teaching?"

"Started again this semester. I've been on a sabbatical for about a year and a half."

"Poor baby. So you didn't break down and go back to the wife."

"Nope. Hey, I have a garden. I'm growing garlic. Just planted it. But I still have a lot from my harvest last July."

"You're beginning to talk like a good old boy. Yeehaw!"

"Listen up, city boy. I still have a few choice tomatoes on the vines. Peppers too. I've put up some mighty fine pesto. Come on up."

"I don't know, man. Just thought about you, said good-bye to my woman, and I'm at loose ends, sort of, but..."

"I'll make you a pasta. My own basil. And garlic bread."

"I'll be there about two o'clock. You have enough garlic for me to take some home? Two or three heads?"

"You got five. Maybe even six."

For the unenlightened:

In the late sixties and early seventies, John Harris had almost single-handedly shocked Americans into an awareness of the neglected glories of garlic. Whenever you read or hear about a garlic festival (and there are about fifty festivals every summer or fall somewhere in the United States), remember that those festivals exist by the grace of John Harris. His self-published *The Book of Garlic* won him local, national, and even international stature as a garlic guru, for the book also appeared in French, Spanish, German, and Japanese. He has been legitimately saluted as the king of garlic.

A few months after my wife and I separated, I met John at a book-signing party. I was taken with his outrageous wit. Over the following months, we met often at the Cheese Board, the first of the Berkeley food collectives, or at Chez Panisse or local cheap cafes. When he offered me an apartment in the basement of his house, I accepted. It was during that time that he initiated me into the daily ritualistic consumption of garlic, which provided me with a distraction from thoughts about my broken marriage. Routed were the armies of resentment, remorse, and guilt that had been attacking me since my escape from the twenty-year marriage.

I can not guarantee the same benefits to other such victims, however.

After I moved out of John's house, he and I continued to run into each other in Berkeley or San Francisco but less frequently. When he called me at the ranch I'd seen him once in the previous three years. But as a memento of our friendship, I had retained my addiction to garlic.

John arrived punctually at two o'clock. Still handsome, and quite fit for a large man. And feisty. I led him to the garden and handed him a spade, which he accepted with palms and fingernails that did not show recent intimacy with the soil.

Giving ourselves to the ceremony with the silent but proud dedication of apostles, we took turns using the spade to loosen the soil and, tugging with our hands, pulled ten heads out of the earth. Like a doting father, John carried our bounty to the back porch. Early on, Dominic had advised me to spread out the stalks in the cool shade for a week or two after harvest.

It had to cure, I informed John, feigning an authority I didn't have or deserve.

"Garlic loses about half of its water while it's curing. Then it's at its best. Whatever is not eaten should be stored, preferably where a cool breeze can get to it."

"Guess what, Chester. I knew all that."

I served linguine with a pesto, made with my own basil, based on Mary Albini's recipe: 3 cups of basil leaves in a blender, virgin olive oil to cover, salt and pepper, a handful of pine nuts, a couple of spoonfuls of grated Parmesan, and *molto* garlic, all blended to the thickness of sour cream.

Also served: a salad of red leaf lettuce and arugula (gifts from Brenda Albini), and the last four tomatoes from my garden. For my garlic bread I relied on a recipe I'd learned from a nurse when I worked at Alta Bates Hospital in Berkeley: Slice a loaf of sour French bread lengthwise; cut each length almost clear through into 3- or 4-inch sections; thoroughly (this is important!) drench the soft dough with a warm brew of olive oil, lots of garlic, salt, and grated pepper, all cooked in a frying pan; let the soaked bread sit, crust-side down, for one hour at room temperature (so the juices go down deep toward the crust); top the bread with grated cheese; place the bread, cheese-side up, under the broiler until the cheese begins to brown. Eat till the platter is empty and wiped dry.

The exact amount of garlic? Your heart's desire. Your heart's benefit. Olive oil? Don't worry about your waist. A waist is a terrible thing to mind.

"This," John said, purring louder than Sadie, "is A+++ garlic bread." He would later promote this recipe in his newsletter, *The Garlic Times*.

We ate the whole loaf before we started on the pasta with pesto.

John had brought grated cheese (imported aged Asiago) from the Cheese Board and, in a red-ribboned bag, two bottles of Italian red wine. I pretended to appreciate them. He didn't have to pretend.

What did I know? My standard for the quality of wine has always been that fluid my father made from dandelion blossoms collected from the fields and stored in brown clay crocks. After the sugared blossoms began to ferment and produce, on the foaming top, a scum crawling with worms, he poured the mash—scum, worms, and all—through a filter of that always-reliable flour sacking. Like a Rothschild dispensing gold coins, my father presented the intensely aromatic golden bouillon to very select visitors. Both of them.

For my health I was denied his so-called wine until after I was thirteen and, being bar mitzvahed, was officially a man. His wine, it could safely be said, would stunt the growth of children. It also cracked the clay crocks.

John and I ate our supper on the wide porch that wrapped around the ranch house. In the fields, in the dying light, sheep and cattle moved with that silent and enviable satisfaction enjoyed only by nonhumans.

After the last glass of wine, John sat up and stretched. No lamps had been turned on inside the house. Our only light came from the crescent moon.

John said he'd better be getting back.

When I brought him his ten stalks of garlic, he tore the head from one stalk. Not taking time to clean the dirt from the root hairs, he simply peeled the outer skin free and pried loose a single clove, which, skinned by teeth and thumbnail, he consumed in three quick bites.

I walked John to his car. "This," he said, breathing against the palm of his hand and inhaling, "this has been a day to remember."

I tossed the nine stalks (and the one head minus one clove) onto the front seat beside John, certain that before he reached Berkeley he would consume most if not all of the remaining cloves in the open head.

CHAPTER 4

Christmas Eve

WHEN JOHN CALLED to thank me for dinner, he asked if I'd ever considered growing garlic commercially. I had to laugh and did.

I told him that given my full-time job at the college and the exhausting drive, and my almost full-time responsibilities at the sheep ranch, I barely even had the time, let alone the energy, to write.

"Write? Romance, mystery, adventure? Jim falls in love with Rosie and they go big-game hunting in Africa and someone shoots Rosie after she's fallen into a hippo pool and Jim rescues her just before a giant crocodile appears? Those stories?"

"That's good! Can I use that?"

"Hey, hey, hey. I forgot. You've published short stories. Last I heard was ... what? ... five years ago. I thought you gave up. Oh yeah, your sabbatical. You probably worked on a novel."

"I didn't give up. I published a story two years ago. Made forty bucks."

"After such impressive remuneration I guess I can't convince you to grow garlic commercially."

"No, I don't think so, John. I'm not a farmer. Who among our friends would be willing to work so hard for so little? And, as you know too well, it's hard work. And besides, for me farming is not a political statement. Isn't everything in Berkeley supposed to be political?"

"If you change your mind, call me. Meantime, I've just made you an honorary member of Lovers of the Stinking Rose. You'll be getting our newsletter every month. And as it says on the masthead, *Allium est, allium best*."

"Same to you, John."

"You gotta say it. It uplifts the spirit. If you can't have the clove in your mouth you can at least have the word."

"*Allium est, allium best,* John."

I didn't see or hear from John again until long after I left the sheep ranch in Bodega and moved to Occidental.

But every so often I received his newsletter, *Garlic Times*, the call to arms of his own garlic-lovers' association, the almost-political Lovers of the Stinking Rose.

Those original fifty cloves of Dominic's garlic went on through ten generations. The tenth was planted in October, 1985, my final autumn at the ranch.

Since I planted a hundred cloves each successive year after my arrival in Bodega (and lost more than half to gophers before each harvest), the harvested inventory always remained at about fifty.

Were it not for the ranch cats, there would have been even more gopher damage. They had been skinny and diseased when I'd arrived at the ranch. Thanks to the plenitude of little rodents that were soon plump from eating my garlic, the cats grew sleek and plump themselves. And untouchable.

Feral cats should always be considered potential enemies. A then-incipient cat lover, I thought one of the creatures, a thin calico tom, especially endearing. I lured him into a very cautious trust. He would let me bend over him when he rushed to eat the kibble. One evening I foolishly reached to pet him. He sank his teeth into the palm of my hand. I had to wave my arm and jerk my wrist to shake him off. He ran off into the high grasses.

The next day my hand was swollen.

I visited Dr. Morton Meyer, my physician in Berkeley. Dr. Meyer insisted that, because Sonoma County was infected with rabies that year, I'd have to start the treatment. Twelve shots in the abdomen, one each day. If I caught the cat and had it tested and it proved to be free of rabies (it would have to be killed and its brain examined), I could stop the shots.

Dominic and I searched for the calico tom, but never found him. The serum of choice in those years was made from duck albumen. The shots were very painful. To complicate matters (and also make me ill), I discovered after the third shot that I was allergic to duck. By then it was too late to change to the other available serum, which was made from the brain tissue of humans who'd died from rabies.

You've heard that writers live to exploit all friends and enemies, all experiences, good or evil. It's true. The young-adult novel I wrote after this experience was called CATCH CALICO!

The other cats, unconcerned about the disappearance of one of their tribe, kept after the gophers.

Every season, Dominic was always peeved because I lost fewer heads of my garlic to gophers, and the surviving heads were consistently larger than his. He couldn't understand. I wasn't even Italian. I was an amateur farmer, even lower than amateur. What was I doing right that he was doing wrong? Was I collecting nicotine juice from Art Casini's bar up the road in Bodega? Was I adding some secret ingredient to my soil?

"Maybe," I told Dominic, "your garlic's angry. You call it a bulb, I call it a head. Calling it a bulb insults it. Garlic is sensitive, you know. Transylvanians play flutes and recorders for their plants every full-moon night."

He didn't think much of my reasoning.

"No wine for you at Christmas," he said.

I almost thanked him but I caught myself. Every time I drank Dominic's homemade wine, it soured my stomach and my dreams, but I always managed to offer appreciative comments.

Maybe, I suggested, we ought to blame the location. This Bodega ranch house was in a valley, sheltered from sea winds and fog. There was more sun and warmth here than at his Valley Ford ranch, which was quite exposed, in its spread across the hills, to the salty coastal winds.

As a test, I gave him several of my largest heads. We both took for granted that they would, in turn, produce large heads for him. But at each harvest his heads consistently remained smaller than mine.

We stopped discussing it.

The day I'd arrived at the Bodega ranch house, Dominic had handed me a box of shells and a rifle. "A thirty-ought-six," he said. "Used it for hunting deer for twenty years."

Upper left: Dukanskij, upper right: Yugoslavian Red, bottom: Brown Tempest.

Upper left: Leningrad, upper right: Spanish Roja, bottom: Rose du Var.

Left: Burgundy, right: Creole Red.

Top: Chet's Italian Red, bottom left: Romanian Red, bottom right: Inchelium Red.

I was to shoot any stray dogs anywhere on the ranch at any time. "Stray dog" meant any dog that was not either one of his collies.

This sounds hard-hearted and cruel. But remember: Dominic is a man whose business is farming. He earns his money working in the fields and barns, not in a high-rise office building or a low-rise shopping mall. He works as hard as his father and his grandfather worked for not a hell of a lot more. Sure, he eats better perhaps, he dresses better. Because he's warned earlier by satellite about weather and because he has more knowledge at hand about the intricacies of ranching-as-business, he can be more alert to natural or commercial hazards and, if lucky, prepare for them in time. He has a '92 Oldsmobile station wagon and a '91 Chevy pickup and, in his Valley Ford home, two television sets. But at night he stands on the porch and studies the sky and worries about the same problems his parents and grandparents had worried about: what sort of world will his children inherit? Will they ever be tempted to leave the hard uncertainties of the land for the soft uncertainties of the city?

Dominic Albini is not a corporate executive with bureaus and levels of functionaries between himself and his final product.

One morning, I woke up at about two o'clock and through my bedroom window saw a bobbing flashlight in the nearby field.

My first thought: *rustlers*.

Several neighbors had reported losses of cattle and sheep to swift and efficient thieves traveling the country roads at night in vans. Justice, should those people be caught, would not be democratic.

Was that a rustler out there in the field?

Like an old-time marshal being paid to do a job, I owed allegiance to Dominic.

After pulling on pants and boots and a jacket, I loaded the rifle, driven by equal portions of anger and reluctance and fear. I did not turn on a light, even when I descended the treacherous stairs leading down to the kitchen. I did take the big three-cell flashlight Dominic had brought me. "You never know," he'd advised me.

I moved as quietly as possible through the dark, cold drizzle to an oak tree about fifteen feet from the bobbing flashlight.

"Who's out there?" I called, praying it would be Mother Teresa.

Dominic's voice: "It's me, Chester. Don't shoot, for God's sake." The beam of my flashlight caught the fluorescent orange of his rain gear. He was on his knees, appearing to be struggling with something. I ran to his side, thinking he might have a coyote by the throat.

A newborn lamb lay in his left arm, curled against his chest. His right hand held a baby bottle.

It's important, when bottle-feeding a lamb, for its head to be tilted up higher than its shoulders so it won't choke. If you watch a lamb rushing to nurse from its mother you'll see the lamb's knees bend, an act that lowers the shoulders, allowing the muzzle to reach up for the ingeniously stationed nipples. That posture clears the esophagus for a straight line to the stomach.

Dominic was having trouble controlling both the tilt of the bottle and the hungry, frightened lamb at the same time. My taking the bottle permitted him to better control the lamb, who, once properly positioned, began to suck and swallow with great intensity.

"The bugger's a runt," Dominic said, pulling the lamb free of the bottle to give it a rest. "Her momma deserted her. I have to take her home. If she dies she'll be warm, at least."

We stayed there for another brief feeding, then Dominic stood up. The smell of wet earth and just-born lamb followed him as, from behind, my flashlight lit his way across the field.

The pickup waited at the fence. Already in the bed of the truck, securely tied to the sideboards, was a ewe with a torn teat, a second ewe with infected and swollen front feet, and her day-old twin lambs.

"That momma with the babies got foot rot. She couldn't walk. She was on her knees, trying to move and take grass while she was down."

"How long have you been here, Dominic? It's about three o'clock."

"Oh, an hour or two."

He wrapped the new lamb in burlap sacks and tucked it down between two boxes so it could not work loose. The other lambs, close to their mother, free for the first time in hours to nurse as they wished, could be trusted to stay close to her. "See you later, Chester. Thanks for being on watch. You earned your keep tonight. Remember to take the shells out of that rifle."

"I can't remember if I put them in."

"Trust me. They're in there."

One more lambing season stands out in my memory: Christmas of 1985, my last at Bodega.

In celebration of the tenth anniversary of our friendship, the Albinis had planned a special Christmas supper. They knew I was a Jew, but they also knew I taught at a Catholic college and so must be fairly accepting. Dominic insisted I be at the supper.

My previous Christmases had been spent with friends in Berkeley or San Francisco or with family in Los Angeles—people who waved indulgent hands at the holiday, seeing it as one more opportunity to prepare elaborate suppers and reunions.

The Albinis had never invited me for a Christmas supper before. Uneasy about protocol, I worked at finding special little inexpensive gifts for everyone. I informed Dominic of my plans because I didn't want them to feel awkward should they have gotten a gift for me. I was expecting one of their usual and very welcome holiday offerings: a haunch of venison from the yearly hunting expedition to Utah or a large fresh salmon or a bottle of drinkable local wine. Never, at Christmas, Dominic's own mean liquid.

"Do you ever eat garlic mashed potatoes?"

"Sounds good, Dominic. I'll bring chicken and matzoh ball soup."

"No, no. You don't have to bring any food. You're our guest. What's a matzoh ball?"

"Matzoh balls come from the male matzohs. Hard to find around Northern California."

"No kidding? You have to hunt them? Where are they?"

"Oh, they're up in the hills."

"I've lived here all my life. Don't believe I've ever seen one. Are they hard to track?"

"Easy. I'm surprised you've never seen them. But you have to remember, only the males have the balls."

"Well, I know that, Chester. You sure you're not talking about Rocky Mountain oysters? I got a freezer full of Rocky Mountain oysters."

"No. These are real matzoh balls."

"Son of a gun. Do you have any of the balls around? In the freezer?"

"No, I only eat fresh balls. I go out before sunrise on Christmas morning. That's the best time to get them."

"You know I love to hunt. I'd go with you, but Christmas morning it's difficult. We go to Mass."

The joke, old as it was, had gone too far. The trusting Dominic was too easy a victim. I finally broke down and told him the truth. Matzoh balls are made with eggs and matzoh meal. The meal is made from ground matzohs, which are crackers. He wasn't peeved at all. In fact, he told me to carry on the whole joke with the family and he'd play along, assuring them that he'd accompanied me when I'd gone hunting for the male matzohs.

Christmas Eve. I could see the mix of early moonlight and light fog through the kitchen window.

The fire in the wood-burning cook stove warmed the first floor of the house, but in the upstairs rooms the windows were coated with frost. I sat at the kitchen table, my back to the stove, listening to the radio and reading the fourth version of a Christmas story I'd begun three years earlier.

There was a knock on the door and I looked up to see the faces of Dominic and Brenda at the window.

They'd brought a ewe down from the hills, Dominic said. She was in one of the stalls in the barn, ready to deliver. But she was having problems, which was why he didn't want her out in the cold, wet hills. She could die. Her lambs could die. Stray dogs could get them all.

"Could you check her about nine o'clock, Chester? If she hasn't delivered, call me. We'll come right over. Is that too late for you?"

"Hell no. I stay up till midnight usually. Sometimes later."

"Well, we all go to midnight Mass. So nine o'clock's good if she's still having troubles. I'll come over and pull the lamb. She's probably got two lambs in there. We can be finished and get home and cleaned up in time to go to midnight Mass."

At 8:30 I put on my jacket and my boots and walked to the barn, bending low against the fierce cold wind. The beam of my flashlight showed the ice-topped grass that was crunching under my boots. The temperature would surely go below freezing tonight. Lucky that ewe, lucky those lambs, to be in relative comfort inside the barn.

I turned on the bulb at the end of the long cord hanging from a rafter. The ewe, rear legs spread, head down, was standing in a corner, leaning against the wall. Her abdomen was swollen about as far as it could go without bursting. The fleece beneath her stubby tail was bright red, but there was no other evidence of impending birth. I talked to her for a few minutes and trudged back to the house, where I worked on my endless novel.

After a stiff shot of Black Bush (to which Donald Fanger, at Harvard, had introduced me), I added several logs to the iron stove and picked up a recent *New Yorker*. At that time, 1985, it was a fine magazine.

About nine o'clock, on my second tour of inspection, the ewe was down, panting and groaning, working hard, exertion shaking her entire body. There was more fluid and blood now—not just on her rear, under the tail, but on the hay. Though her vaginal lips were swollen there was still no evidence of a protruding head.

I called Dominic. Twenty minutes later he and Brenda and Suzie arrived, all three bundled up against the cold. Marty and his mother had stayed home, at the Valley Ford ranch, where two ewes were having similar troubles.

Dominic backed the pickup to the barn door and got out. Brenda and Suzie hurried into the almost-warm barn. Dominic hauled an extension cord from one of the many little side rooms and rigged up a small but powerful spotlight, which he clamped onto the top board of the stall. He focused the light on the ewe. As the four of us entered the stall the ewe tried to rise and run, but Brenda and Suzie dug their fingers into the wool to restrain her.

"Chester," Dominic said, "would you help Brenda and Suzie hold her down?"

While the three of us were restraining the ewe, Dominic removed his heavy jacket, sprayed soap on his hands, and washed them with water from a jug he'd brought from the truck. He dried his hands on a clean towel and then pulled on a long pair of rubber gloves taken from a sealed bag. The ewe groaned and bucked as Dominic, on his knees, thrust his right gloved hand inside her.

"What I thought," Dominic said. "Crossways."

"Tonight of all nights," Brenda complained. "I bet it's the same at Valley Ford."

"I'll have to try to turn the little bugger around," Dominic said, reaching in again. Dominic talked to the protesting ewe, calling her Momma and Little Mother, and apologized for hurting her. "Can't get hold of the feet," he said. "They're slippery. If I can get the feet I can maybe turn it around enough to pull it out. Nope, my hands are too big. You try, Sis."

Even though it was near freezing outside the thin walled barn, here, in the stall, the four of us were sweating, converting the confined space into a steam bath.

Brenda washed her hands and arms and carefully donned the gloves her father had used. Dominic and Suzie and I restrained the ewe while Brenda worked. "Can't turn it," she said. "But I got the feet. Nope, they slipped back."

She tried for another ten minutes, grimacing, almost weeping, at every protest from the ewe.

"Stop," Dominic said. "No use putting her through any more misery. I could cut her open but I haven't had much luck lately. Been getting infections. Losing lambs as well as mommas. What time is it? Must be about ten. Should have called the vet. It's too late now. Anyway, he'd just be at some other ranch. Or at church. Well, I hate to do this to you, Momma."

He went to the truck bed and returned with a rope. "Sis, see can you get those feet out just a bit." He kneeled at the side of the ewe where Brenda had been struggling.

After working for a few minutes, Brenda finally had the shiny black hooves exposed. "Now. Do it, do it, Daddy."

Dominic knotted the rope around the two barely visible hooves that were covered with soft gristle so they'd not tear the mother's gut.

I thought of Blake's poem: *"Tyger, tyger, burning bright ... did He who made the lamb make thee..."*

Yes, He did.

Without the aid of a computer or the AMA, He had designed the lamb's hooves to protect the walls of the mother's womb. Man, however, had designed rope and truck.

"Oh God," Suzie said, "I hate this. Please, Daddy. Not tonight."

"Have to," Dominic said.

He looked as if he were in pain himself. He moved the pickup forward until the rope grew taut.

"Slow," Brenda called. "Slow, Daddy."

The truck inched ahead. Snorting and bucking under my body, the ewe threw me so high in the air I could hardly keep my hold on her head and shoulders. Then, following a sound like a sink drain unclogging, a lamb popped out onto the hay, followed by a flow of blood and afterbirth. As Dominic continued to move the truck forward Brenda and Suzie and I screamed, "Stop! Stop!"

Dominic pulled on the handbrake, leaped from the cab of the pickup and rushed back into the barn. Brenda was already untying the ropes. Dominic, lying flat, put the lamb's muzzle into his own mouth. He turned his head to the side each time he inhaled. Then, clutching the lamb's tiny head, he continued to pump new air into its lungs.

As if it were a signal to its mother's womb, the moment the lamb gave a little cough and choked and coughed again and began breathing on its own, another whoosh of blood swept out a second lamb. This time Brenda performed the mouth-to-mouth until the second lamb coughed, gagged, coughed again, and began to breathe on its own.

Dominic wiped the nose of the ewe across the backs of both lambs. She was so still I thought she might be dead.

"Imprint," Suzie said, as if I didn't already know. "She'll be able to pick these two out of the whole herd now."

A few minutes passed. None of us spoke. Then the ewe shivered. She shook her body, lifted her head and, after several tries, with help from Dominic and me, she managed to stand. Brenda wiped the nose of each lamb across the ewe's teats.

"Now," Suzie, the conscientious teacher, informed me, "they'll be able to find her anywhere."

The lambs, crying, climbed onto their own weak legs. They fell over, pulled themselves upright, fell again and then, somewhat stabilized, they began their search. Suzie said, "No, no," when I reached to help them. "The work makes them stronger."

Finally one lamb and then the other, after searching under the tail and under the ears and under the front legs, found two teats, found two nipples, began to suck.

"Let's go home," Brenda said.

Dominic patted my shoulder. "Chester, thanks a lot. Merry Christmas. I'll check her again after Mass. You see a truck in front of the barn, don't shoot. It'll be me."

I watched the truck's taillights move along the dirt road but I remained there, in the barnyard, inhaling the cold crisp wind. The stars had never in my entire life seemed brighter, had never ridden so close to the earth.

I could not help thinking of my first and only midnight Mass.

It had been in Pennsylvania, where I'd grown up with Catholic and Protestant kids. There, in North Butler, a coal mine village, the Christmas crèche under the tree in Jimmy Stroble's house, in Roman's house, in Goose's battered shack of a home, in Johnny Prebula's house, contained homemade miniatures: finger-sized cattle and sheep and tiny white lambs carved from balsa wood.

I'd gone with Johnny Prebula and Jimmy Stroble and Goose to midnight Mass in town. The color and pageantry and music provoked sad longing. As the organ music swelled and the priest sang out in Latin and the congregation and choir responded, I seriously considered converting to Catholicism.

The following day, however, when I received my first of seven nights of Chanukah gifts, I was quite satisfied with being a Jew.

Now it was another Christmas Eve. I realized, on this Bodega night, why the lamb has become a symbol for tranquillity, for innocence. Even a hardened man can be reduced to tears when he holds a newborn lamb in his arms.

"Peace on earth," the carolers sang, on that Christmas Eve in our little impoverished mining town in Pennsylvania.

Goodwill to men.

There were no carolers this night in Bodega.

I wanted to go into the ranch house and find my cassette of Frederica Von Stade singing Christmas hymns: an angelic voice, suitable for the Savior and His wisest men.

Had there been a bible available I would certainly have read it. Well, at least the Old Testament.

I rested on the porch and drank a glass of wine. I'd probably come down with a serious cold sitting like this, I thought, my clothes soaked, the wind bitter. I couldn't have cared less.

Back at the barn, close to midnight, I found both lambs standing up. Their legs were trembling but the lambs looked quite likely to survive. The mother had already licked them clean. Shaking their heads, flicking their ears, they were trying to hop about. Each fell over several times but stumbled upright to hop again, to fall over and stand again.

Two people were with me: William Blake, and my ex-wife.

She would have enjoyed this night. She was Irish, and had been a Catholic child—a beautiful but also potentially ferocious combination that had always enhanced, for the best and the worst, every emotion I'd experienced during my marriage.

In the ranch house, now quite sleepy, I called Mary Catherine O'Connor, whom I'd met several months before at a dinner in San Francisco. One Sunday just after Thanksgiving, she'd visited me at Bodega.

Mary Catherine wasn't home.

I left a message. "It's about an hour past Christmas Eve. Tonight, just before midnight, I helped midwife the birth of twin lambs. Babies and mother doing well. I'm glad you're not home to curse me for waking you up. There are approximately fifty million other women in California, maybe a fourth of them named Mary. Why, I wonder, did I feel the need to call you?"

What is it about Jewish men and Irish women?

I was asleep when, after Mass, Dominic returned to check on the sheep.

Following our Christmas supper Dominic said he wanted to talk to me. We carried our glasses of Gallo wine (thank God!) out onto the porch.

"Chester, Suzie's getting married in March. I didn't know this when I invited you for supper."

"And she'll be moving into the ranch house. Of course. It's been a joy these past nine years, Dominic. Suzie deserves to live there."

"You won't have to leave right away. Might be later than March before they move into the house. Gotta line up workers to do some remodeling. If they can't get to it you might be able to stay until July. Maybe even August."

"That's plenty of time to prepare. Living there has been a gift, Dominic. So has your friendship. I'll thank you, all of you, as long as I live."

"Till you're a hundred, if you keep eating garlic. I could have waited a while before telling you, but I thought, well, I was sure you'd understand."

"Believe me, Dominic. I understand. It's about time for me to move on, anyway. I began a new life here. I ought to continue it. Or maybe start another new life."

He laughed. "We sure had them going with that matzoh ball story, didn't we?"

We had, indeed.

"You know," Dominic said, "Even after you leave you keep coming back. Whenever you want. Maybe we can hunt some more male matzohs."

"I have to tell you," I said. "There's one thing I don't understand."

"What's that?"

"I forgot to put garlic in my matzoh ball soup, but it was delicious anyway. Just about the best I've ever made. Hate to say this, but it was even better than my mother's soup."

Dominic shuffled about and cleared his throat several times. "Well, I tasted that soup while it was heating up, Chester. It tasted flat. So I squeezed in ten cloves of California Late and stirred it up."

"Dominic, you bugger."

He shook his head. "Chester, I'm gonna miss you. Neither Suzie or her man cares much for garlic. Of course, he's not Italian. I'm afraid to ask where his parents or grandparents are from. It might be Germany. Or worse yet, England. I don't understand about Suzie. She holds her nose when there's garlic at the table. Maybe she ain't my daughter. Let's go in. I'm freezin' my matzoh balls out here."

CHAPTER 5

Ah, But I Was So Much Older Then

WHEN I'D APPLIED FOR A POSITION at Saint Mary's College in 1967, my having published a novel (which earned me about three thousand dollars) and several prize-winning stories (about two hundred dollars total) had won me an appointment in the English Department. I only had a B.A. at the time. To improve my chances for tenure, which would mean job security, I reluctantly agreed to earn an M.A.

Imagine. Finally, at the age of fifty, to have job security.

Before my appointment to Saint Mary's, I'd worked in hospitals for twenty years and before that in a variety of jobs that included factories and steel mills and parking lots. During and after I began teaching, I lived and worked on the sheep ranch at Bodega.

My colleagues, residents of the academic world since they were teenagers, considered me an interesting but somewhat eccentric mutant. I knew little or nothing about so-called scholarship, and I'd proved, to the satisfaction of myself and my students, that a Ph.D. was not required to be an accomplished or competent or even celebrated teacher. The other instructors smiled and patted my head, as a dog breeder might indulge an old, stray, flea-bitten mutt.

Being a professor required that I *teach*. In other words, reading assigned texts and student papers, and meeting with students to cajole, provoke, threaten, or praise them into...what?...Let's say learning. The term *educate* belongs in there somewhere.

In my freshman writing class I often insisted that the students write about something completely outside the usual list of standard composition topics. I wanted them to struggle with material or experiences foreign to them and to their generation, such as old age or German cabaret music or riding sidesaddle. To pass, they had to use the library for research, which meant they had to enter the library, which meant they had to find it on the campus map, which meant they had to be able to distinguish north from south.

Exasperated one day at the predictability of their boring incompetence and/or disinterest, I blurted out, "Garlic! Write about garlic!"

The students stared at me.

"I want research! I want originality! I want imagination! I want clear, precise, correctly written prose. I want to say, 'I wish I'd written this paper.' Give me three pages."

Two of the twenty papers were quite well written and provocative enough to receive a B and a B+. From one of those two (written by a daughter of a Gilroy garlic farmer) I even learned several tricks about the marketing of garlic, and a few facts about family stability.

Six of the remaining eighteen papers consisted of the history of garlic, all taken, I presume, from the one agriculture encyclopedia in the library. The authors had tiptoed so close to plagiarism I warned them that a grade of C was a gift. Three of the remaining twelve papers were exactly the same, word for word. Each of the three writers had spelled garlic *garlick* and two of the three papers had been submitted under the same name, meaning that the "authors" even copied the original writer's name. Each of those three papers received an F. The other papers received grades ranging from D to C+.

But three of the D papers contained appealing recipes for dishes served in the students' homes. I immediately tried them at Bodega. Knowing I would go on to include them in my permanent collection, I eventually, before the end of the semester, informed each of the three students why I was changing their D to a C-.

I made copies of the three papers and offer here the recipes as written. At the end of each, I present my slight alterations, if any.

Brusell Sprout

Tak some brusell sprout and cut of root end. Cut in haf. Put in Fry pan. Put in littl olive oil. Put in sharp sweat mustard. Put in hot peppr jely. Mix up. Covur and steem til tendr. You cook them to long they go to soft. Serve hot. You got to like brusell sprout of corse. Put in garlick but not to much.

Do as suggested, but keep testing the sprouts with a fork. The mustard I use is a sharp Dijon, with honey added. If you can find Jack Daniel's mustard, use it! I use jalapeño jelly when possible or a cherry or berry jelly with hot pepper flakes added. The amount of all ingredients should be to your taste. Garlic? Use a light hand here, or you'll overwhelm the mustard-jelly taste. Because I was familiar at the time only with California White garlic, I used it. Now I use Inchelium Red from Washington, or Yugoslavian, which is hot at first but mellows to a pleasant aftertaste. Allow 4 to 5 brussels sprouts per person.

Humus

Humus is made from chikpese. My granfathr comes from Lebanon and they eat lots of humus there. But its a lot of work my mom say. So she buys it from a markit in San Francisco sells things like Lebanon stuff. Then before we get it on the tabl my mother who like garlick a lot squeezes in a lot of garlick. I mean lotz. You eat my mom's humus you got to like garlick

---

Unlike my student's mother, I make my own hummus (garbanzo beans, tahini, olive oil, lemon juice). For each two cups I add 5 or 6 cloves of a garlic that's not too (pardon me, I mean to) hot, such as a Spanish Roja or a French Messadrone. If you like biting hot, use 2 or 3 cloves of the standard California White garlic, or, even better, 2 or 3 cloves of one of the Georgian garlics. Their heat disappears fast, and a very strong, earthy garlic taste remains. I do not chop or dice or slice the garlic; I use a garlic press.

Galic Omlet

You like eggs a lot you take 3 eggs. You don't like eggs a lot you take two. Brake them. In a fring pan. Throw cells away. Befor you throw eggs in pan you throw them in a bole. You stir them with a fork. You add rosemary. Thats a herb. My dad grows it. You also add salt&pepper. You take three slices bread you use three eggs two slices bread you use two eggs. You break the slices bread into pices. You soak these pices in butter. Now you add lots garlick. My dad uses butter and olive oil half half. You add these soaked pices into bowl thats got your eggs stirrd. You pore everytheng in to hot fring pan that has a little oil. Olive. Fry. Stir. Let sit till side on bottom gets brown. Flip. Fry until that side now on bottom gets brown. Flip. Put on plate. Eat. Right away.

What can I say? I make this omelet for breakfast or for lunch. The garlic I use here is either Spanish Roja or Creole Red, for the rich, rich taste. Use Mexican or Polish Carpathian Red or Leningrad, and you'll do a double flip. Roast 4 or 5 cloves of garlic and add it to the whipped eggs, and your flips will be of Olympic proportions. Just wrap the cloves in foil (after removing their tips), cover them with olive oil, and bake for 45 minutes at 350°.

My late-in-life obsession with garlic developed slowly, but with an intensity that sometimes gave me pause. Too often in my life my obsessions—with writing, with teaching, with politics (and sometimes teaching and politics combined), with isolation—have stuffed my emotional baggage with explosives.

But garlic calmed me down. Starting with Mary Albini's garlic mashed potatoes and, almost accidentally, my students' recipes for garlic brussels sprouts, garlic omelet, and garlic hummus.

Garlic made my life ideal.

But so has the land.

Let's call it nature.

There have been days and nights when I have felt so possessive of these trees and meadows and birds and animals that I wanted to lie down on the ground and embrace the entire endangered planet.

Though I did not fool myself into thinking that I was a pioneer, or beyond the control of tradition, I began to appreciate those qualities in this piece of Northern California that had attracted the pioneers. More importantly, I began to appreciate the love of the Native Americans for this sacred land, a love that had compelled them to resist and resent the theft of it by the pioneers.

At the sheep ranch, I occasionally laid out my sleeping bag on the battered old porch, close to the wall, and savored the sounds and smells of the fields. I was watched over by the moon that had ridden the skies over Poland and Russia when my parents had been born. When I shiver with the stars and smell the ocean on the breeze, I can only bless my good fortune. I resist the need to go inside, to turn out the lights, to go to bed.

Standing on one of those hills that surround the ranch house, sweeping my binoculars over the meadows and boulders in search of crippled ewes or stranded lambs, I could, by slightly adjusting my binoculars, see the Pacific Ocean. When the dark rains swept in from the sea and the cattle and sheep patiently accepted their fate for hours or days or weeks, even then I moved through the trees and high grasses with an almost primitive tranquillity.

Compelled, because of work or social obligations, to be in the streets or cafes of Berkeley or San Francisco, or on Saint Mary's campus, I struggled to be civil. The clash of terrors and frustrations promised a despair as final, as painful, as a fatal disease. Old friends I'd once considered sophisticated ranted and raved their way through what appeared to me to be trivial activities. As if darkness would be falling at noon.

Depressed by campus politicking and national and international atrocities, in shock at the deaths of four of my six brothers, I found distraction by walking the Bodega hills, caring for sick or injured sheep. I chased off dogs by firing my rifle over their heads. With a sledge and wedges I split oak and manzanita rounds (supplied by Dominic) into sticks for the kitchen's iron stove. I never failed to put in an hour or two every day on the novel I was writing. And, of course, I planted and tended my garden, and harvested.

Always attendant was the ghost of my father, stepping out from behind a tree or appearing in the grasses.

Each year, year after year, I planted and harvested and ate more garlic.

Why did I plant the garlic the last year I lived at the ranch, even though I'd be leaving before I could harvest it? I did not plant a single tomato or carrot or pepper. Not even one basil plant. Just the garlic. One hundred and fifty cloves in the usual circle.

One hundred and fifty sentinels guarding nothing.

I knew that Dominic would continue caring for the garlic after I left, I knew he'd harvest it, and I knew he'd call me, wherever I might be, so I could collect my share.

I thought about this compulsive need to finger the garlic heads, to break the heads into cloves, to caress each clove and set it to bed in the damp soil. I thought about it then and I've thought about it since.

On our exchange of visits, Dominic and I performed our little dance of competition. The truth is, Dominic's garlic would never be as robust as mine. At the time, I didn't know why.

At the time.

I'm wiser now. And younger, somehow.

Dominic and Suzie granted me an extension because the men who were to work on the house would not be available on the date they'd promised.

In May, I sold my house in Bolinas and found myself with money in the bank.

At the age of sixty-two, with three more years to teach, I was about to start, again, a new life.

I called a realtor and we went to work. "If it's land," I told her, "it has to be land with potential building sites. If it's a house, it has to have meadows and trees around it."

Over the next four weeks, Teresa Patterson showed me several houses and several parcels of land.

Something was always wrong. The house was too new, or too decrepit, the site was too hilly, or too flat. There were no trees, there were too many trees. The soil would not perk, meaning it would not take a septic system, or there was no promise of adequate water, meaning it had an unreliable well or no well at all.

I was about to give up, thinking that I would have to rent an apartment in Sebastopol or Santa Rosa, when one Sunday evening in early September, before classes began at the college, Teresa called me at the ranch.

"There's a five-acre site in Occidental going on the market Tuesday morning. If you offer some honest money, say five hundred dollars, it's yours. I'll call the other realtor tonight. She's a friend."

The realtor picked me up an hour later. We drove past a struggling vineyard onto a rutted dirt road. "This road might need some work," she said.

My doubts sprang alive.

She forced the car under a dense canopy of oak and redwood trees and through a surreal web of blackberry bushes. Five miles an hour.

My heart continued sinking. This was not looking good.

Then, bright sunlight.

She stopped at a wooden gate that hung by a single rusted hinge. She gestured at the sunburned meadows, the stands of huge redwoods. "This is it."

Meadow, redwoods, gentle slopes, sun. Lots of sun.

I tried to perfect the role of someone who has been visiting Eden twice every day and is no longer impressed. Ecstasy is a bore.

I began to lose it as we walked the land.

From the side of the road the meadow sloped very gently down to a sizable grove of redwoods. Deep inside the grove we found what had once been a fence. That was the western border. The northern border was another grove of redwoods that rose so high the flat piece of field in front of them lay in late afternoon shade. In the morning and through much of the day the site would be in filtered sunlight.

"Nice site for a house," the realtor said. "That was the site selected by the seller."

Marked by rows of faded red flags, the site, she informed me, was at a legal distance from the septic system. "The septic system and the well were installed a year ago. Everything's up to code."

"What about the well?"

"Tested at seven-gallons-a-minute recovery during the drought. Better than average. Probably nine- or ten-a-minute after the rains. Pretty damn good. Not great, but good. Good enough for garlic."

"Have you ever grown garlic?"

"No."

The young owners who'd gone so far as to have plans drawn up for their house had been prepared to live here the rest of their lives. Some unexplained disaster had destroyed their dreams. That was the extent of Teresa's information.

Back at the road, we leaned against the car. Before me, scattered across the western slope, almost hidden within the tall golden grasses, were nine pear and apple trees, a few fruits still clinging to twisted limbs.

"Those trees are probably forty years old," she said.

"Wait till they really get old," I said. "They'll produce twice as much as they do now."

I was trying to muster my detached cynicism, trying to act like a tough client who still had questions to ask and standards to meet, when out of the western redwoods came two deer—a doe and a six-point buck. The real owners, patrolling their land.

They continued up through the meadow, pausing under an apple tree to sample a few windfalls lying in the grass. A hummingbird whirred past my ear to settle on a nearby bush of lavender.

"You arranged this whole scene," I said. "It's cheap Hollywood."

She smiled. "It is more beautiful than I'd imagined."

"I want it."

"So do I. But you get it, damn it. If I'd seen the place before I brought you, you'd not be here."

CHAPTER 6

The Late Beginning of It All

SUZIE ALBINI, CONVINCED THAT her marriage would not be blessed with good fortune were I turned out of the ranch house too quickly, had insisted I remain at Bodega until the workmen were prepared to start on the remodeling. Fortunately, their not meeting the deadline gave me extra months of relaxation.

Suzie's firm belief that her marriage would be endangered were she to turn me out before I had my own home to go to did not seem at all like a silly superstition to me. Who was I to treat such metaphysical superstitions with disdain? Hadn't I, for the last ten years, appreciated and even relied on my conversations with my long-dead mother and father?

Suzie's attempts to ensure the fate of her marriage meant I was not compelled to rent motel rooms or beg for beds from friends in Berkeley or San Francisco as the piles of lumber on my land in Occidental gradually took on the shape of a house.

I stayed at the Bodega ranch through that summer, walking the hills and spending the long evenings trying to add pages to my novel. Often, when I drove to Occidental to oversee the construction of my home, I ate supper at the Union Hotel, which was owned by the sixth generation of the Gonella family.

Over a century ago the immigrant Gonellas, along with the Negris and Panizerras and Fioris, had established hotels and restaurants in Occidental for the hundreds of other Italian immigrant families who had come to Northern California to search out a better life than could then be found in impoverished Italy. These peasant men and women worked long hours every day cutting timber, producing charcoal, and establishing their own gardens and orchards and vineyards. On Saturday nights, families from twenty to thirty miles away rode in carts to the three Italian restaurants in Occidental for food and wine, as well as for information about both the new and the old country.

Today, for most of the descendants of those Italians peasants, the old country and its language and culture are as foreign as the culture of New York City, three thousand miles to the east. Or even San Francisco, sixty miles to the south. The old-country hospitality, however, continues. All meals—sumptuous, earthy, inexpensive—are served with a cordiality and generosity that only the French would scorn.

Dominic, once or twice with the family, several times alone, visited me at Occidental as my house took shape. One evening in the last month of construction, the entire Albini family appeared, unannounced, with a basket of sandwiches, bottles of beer and wine. And Mary's chocolate cake.

Commandeering a few rough benches the carpenters used for their coffee breaks and lunches, we sat on the span of deck that reached out from the northwest corner of the house into the shade of the giant redwoods.

"You have enough garlic to plant in October?" Dominic asked.

"I might have to get some from you, Dominic. I only have about ten heads left, and they'll be gone before October."

"I'll get some extra garlic from my cousin in Gilroy and we'll check for a night two days into the new moon. Want me to come help you get your first crop in?"

I thanked Dominic and said I'd learned enough by now to be able to accomplish that part of the work myself. He said he'd thought about giving me a couple of sheep to keep down the grass in the lower field, but Marty had reminded him I'd have to build a thousand dollars worth of fencing first.

"Any idea yet where you want to plant your garlic?" Dominic asked.

I pointed out a potential site on the west side of the house, a gentle slope about thirty feet from the part of the deck we were sitting on. It was beyond the shade of the trees, and open to the sun. I wouldn't need a big patch. Fifty cloves would be plenty. About five heads.

Did I think that was enough to hold me over till my harvest in June?

More than enough, I said. I offered to pay him.

He was almost offended. Anyway, he said, if he gave me the garlic he'd feel free to call me if he needed help with the sheep. "You got a good well?"

"Not great, but good enough. Seven gallons refill per minute."

Did the water have iron? Sulfur?

"Both. Actually, I used a neighbor's bathroom the other day. His toilet bowl and tub are crusted with rust."

"You might have to get a water processor. They're expensive. Cheapest is around a thousand dollars."

"I better not retire," I said.

"Marry a rich woman," Mary Albini put in, as she sliced the cake.

"I better keep working *and* marry a rich woman."

Marty, usually even shyer and quieter than his mother, murmured, "Find one for me while you're at it."

I met Alison Dykstra at the Union Hotel restaurant one day and in our conversation discovered we not only shared a cynical view of the institution called marriage but also a moderately restrained interest in the ecology movement.

Alison was the director of the Farallones Institute, which occupied a site of about forty acres in the hills above Occidental. A changing population of fifty to sixty people, energetic and idealistic young men and women who practiced an Americanized Zen version of saving the earth, were experimenting with a communal life that, they hoped, would enrich humanity spiritually and the land physically. They had organized a serious study of building designs (rustic but almost elegant solar houses) and building materials (concrete, glass, redwood, adobe), as well as techniques for harnessing the power of so-called alternative energy systems, meaning sun, wind, and water.

On the day of my visit, an acre of varied gardens was being watered by a drip irrigation system designed by Robert Kourik, who won me over with his sense of humor, meaning it was, in its unrestrained but bitter bite, a somewhat sordid reflection of my own.

Alison's tour included one of the solar houses in which, as assistant director, she'd been living for three years. The house, just large enough for one person, had been designed by the Institute's architect.

The south wall of floor-to-ceiling double-glazed windows admitted so much light and warmth that Alison was compelled to use the iron stove tucked into a corner on only the darkest, wettest, coldest days. She walked me through the system's technology, describing how the sun was used to both heat the house in cold weather and cool it during the hot days of summer.

"I want this same house," I said. "But two or three times larger. I have friends and family who'll be visiting me."

"The architect's here. Come meet him."

I met Peter and an agreement was made on the spot.

In my visits to Occidental during construction I'd only seen my deer a few times. *My deer.* The noise and activity during construction had obviously frightened them onto other, more distant meadows.

Mary Catherine and I had visited my land at dusk four times during construction, after the pounding and sawing had stopped for the day.

On the fourth visit, a late summer evening, we stretched out beneath a pear tree, intending to observe the coming of what we both now termed *the light*. The sun, in the last moment of retreat, carried off pieces of our clothing.

In each other's arms, neither of us wanted to make the first move to return to the car and drive back to Bodega.

"Look," Mary Catherine whispered.

A bird was flying slowly across the face of the moon, its black body straight, its great wings rising lazily up and down.

"In Gaelic folklore that's supposed to mean good luck."

I was impressed with her knowledge until she laughed and admitted, "What I know about Gaelic folklore would fill a gnat's ear."

About two years after I moved into my house, in early November, Robert Kourik gave me forty-four cloves of garlic he'd just received from a friend in Iowa. These forty-four cloves represented six different varieties of garlic. Each variety (two represented by full heads, four by a collection of separate cloves) was in its own paper bag.

On the exterior of each bag, Robert's friend, using a black felt-tipped pen, had identified the variety of garlic enclosed. None of the cloves were white. The colors of the outer skins varied from pink to dark red; a few had purple stripes that showed through the outer skin. Each of the full heads was almost as large as my fist, and the cloves were larger than my thumb.

I had to taste one clove from each, of course, before I planted any of them. I assumed all six would taste the same as my California garlic. Actually Dominic's California garlic.

When I bit off the pointed end of the first naked clove, a prompt, moderately sharp barb struck my tongue and then, in five or ten seconds, faded. My tongue and cheeks had not been scalded as they would have been had the clove been a California White, Early or Late.

After the sting leveled off, the taste that followed brought to mind a memory of dark woods, and my father and me walking there in search of beefsteak mushrooms.

The bite of the second variety lasted longer but seemed to search for the back of my throat, not my cheeks or tongue or palate. It, too, faded fast.

Each of the remaining four varieties differed in the intensity of bite as well as when and where it struck. Once it stopped at my lips. Even my palate, of very limited talent, could distinguish an obvious difference in the taste of each of the garlics once its bite wore off.

My tasting of six cloves meant I had thirty-eight cloves to plant, which I did the very next day.

I did not mention my gift to Dominic, and soon after I'd planted the cloves, I forgot about them. Or rather, I chose not to think about them—there was something almost threatening about those garlics and the uncertainties they posed.

At Robert's advice, in mid-June through mid-July, as the leaves of the California garlic inherited from Dominic and of the varieties from Robert's friend began to turn brown, I stopped watering. The leaves turned brown at different rates. In June, when one or two varieties were brown and ready for harvest, two or three others were still quite green. Over a period of six or seven weeks, as more and more of the green on the leaves gave way to brown, I dug up the little beauties.

After all the garlics had been pulled, I made some calculations. Out of Dominic's fifty-five cloves, I harvested twenty-four. The gophers had taken the other thirty-one. Of Robert's thirty-eight, I harvested thirty-one. The gophers had taken the other seven.

All of the heads of Robert's garlics were larger by half than the largest California, and their skin colors, after the heads were cleared of mud and the outer skins removed, suggested not so much garlic as plums. A garlic called Spanish Roja had cloves protected by a dark red skin that came off with a squeeze of thumb and forefinger. Free of its skin, the clean garlic clove looked exactly like a clove of California garlic, though about twice the size. When I tasted the raw garlic, my eyes teared up at the hot bite, but then the bite slipped away and I thought I was eating some exotic fruit.

I called Robert and asked him where the hell he had gotten those garlics.

"From David Cavagnaro at Seed Savers Exchange in Iowa. He's an old buddy. But each bag was identified. You didn't lose them, did you?"

"I threw them away."

He was furious. "So you don't know which is which or which is where?"

"I'm kidding you. Of course I know. I made six ID tags, one for each variety. Five of the six are from the Republic of Georgia. They fought off the gophers better than the California garlic did."

"That was just luck," Robert said. "Gophers don't speak Georgian."

"I have a favorite."

"What's it called?"

"Russian Red Toch."

Robert, who never loses anything, said he'd try to find David's letter from nine months before. He called me back an hour later. "It's called Russian Red Toch because it's from a village in Soviet Georgia called...I don't know how you say this..."

"Tochliavari?"

"I guess so. Yeah, that's it. How the hell did you know?"

"My father was born near Tochliavari. And his father and his father's father."

"You are kidding me."

"I kid you not."

"Okay, so five are from Georgia. What's the sixth?"

"Spanish Roja. Roja means red and the skin is indeed red."

"Taste?"

"What can I say without betraying my father? Well, I can say it was almost as rich as the Russian Red Toch."

During the summer, while the garlic was drying in my house, I treated the Red Toch with care, rationing my use of the cloves, relying primarily on my store of California White. My strong desire to eat all of the Red Toch was in terrible conflict with my need to save it all. As long as it survived I could see and touch it, could, whenever I passed through the kitchen, caress it with my fingertips.

The large head, with its rose skin, was just too important to my evolving curiosity and respect for my own history. A clove of Red Toch, eaten during a late supper on the deck, intensified my sense of my own history.

Plant this garlic? Feed even a clove, let alone a head, to those vicious gophers? No! I had to save it all!

In October, when it was time again for the garlic to go into the ground, I planted the California but kept back the Georgians and the Roja. I just could not bring myself to part with them.

In November, I began to worry. It was almost too late to plant any garlic for the next summer's harvest, and stricken at the discovery, I was finding a few Red Toch cloves now—as well as an occasional Rosewood or a Georgian Crystal or a Zemo—that had begun to rot.

If the remaining garlics were to be available next year, they had to go into the ground now. Immediately.

Of the seven heads of Red Toch I still had, I could plant six. Eight or nine cloves to a head meant I would probably have forty-five fit to go into the ground. If the same survival rate as the first planting continued, I would have about forty heads next summer.

Forty heads of garlic from the Georgian village of Tochliavari, where my life began.

Even if the gophers had built a resistance to the almost magic resistance of the Red Toch and took as many as ten, I'd have many more than I'd had before or had now.

Chance it?

Chance it.

At Robert's advice I called David Cavagnaro in Iowa.

"Glad to hear from any friend of Robert's. Red Toch? No problem. I'll send you three more heads."

"You did say heads. You don't mean *cloves?*"

"Heads. Some people call them bulbs. Do you want a few other varieties? How about a French garlic called Messadrone? And one called Creole Red. Oh, and my personal favorite: Inchelium Red. I'll send along a couple other Georgians, too. You'll get them in about four days. Don't waste time. Get them in the ground immediately."

My head was spinning. I called Robert. Could he, when the garlic arrived, give me a hand? "I'm scared to do it myself."

"Scared of what?" Robert asked.

"Of fouling up. Of losing them *all* to gophers. I remember what you said."

"What did I say and when did I say it?"

"You said I was just lucky that the gophers only took a few heads. I've already put Dominic's California garlic in the ground, but I'll plant my Georgian garlics and the new varieties David Cavagnaro has promised as soon as they arrive. You're the expert. Help!"

"I remember. Your father was born in Cashandcarry, or wherever it was."

"Tochliavari. Georgia."

"Well, to fight the gophers we better plant them all in boxes."

"A box. Any kind of box?"

"No. You make a box of redwood 2 x 12s, with half-inch mesh chicken wire on the bottom. That'll keep out gophers. I'm going to town in an hour. I'll take my pickup truck. I'll get the materials—redwood, chicken wire, staples—and come by your house afterward and we'll build the boxes. If..."

"Go on. If?"

"If you let me take photos from the time we build the boxes through next summer's harvest. I might want to write an article."

"Done."

"You better call Grab & Grow and order soil. Enough for two boxes. About three cubic yards. Get their garden mix. These garlics will probably need more nutrients and tilth than your hardpan soil can give them. After the soil's down we'll do a test for pH."

Tilth? Hard Pan? pH? What the hell was he talking about?

I didn't want to take Robert's time on the phone to have him define the new vocabulary, which I'd probably have to learn eventually, but I was beginning to realize that I just might be graduating from the elementary, almost primitive, act of simply dropping cloves into the soil to a new and sophisticated occupation called *farming*.

Working on someone else's ranch part-time, as a lark, with no real responsibilities, was one thing. Working for myself, on my own ranch, or farm, with the possibility of failure, was another.

"Robert?"

"Yeah?"

"The soil probably won't get here until the day after tomorrow. After we build the boxes this afternoon can you help me for just an hour or two the day the soil arrives? I'll get it in the boxes myself, before you get here, but I'd like to watch you get the planting started."

"You'll invite me to supper?"

"Done. Well, will be done."

"Use lots of garlic. I have to taste that Tokalilivoovoo."

CHAPTER 7

Drip Irrigation and Soil Exams

FOUR DAYS AFTER MY PHONE CALL, UPS delivered a parcel (about twice the size of a shoebox) from David Cavagnaro at Seed Savers Exchange in Decorah, Iowa.

There were eleven paper bags, some containing one or two or even three full heads of garlic, some a handful of cloves. The identity and the amount of the garlic in each bag had been written on the brown paper in neat script with a black felt-tipped pen:

Russian Red Toch (Georgia)	*3 heads*
Medidzhvari (Georgia)	*1 head*
La Panant Kari (Georgia)	*12 cloves*
Korean Rocambole (Korea)	*9 cloves*
Messadrone (France)	*1 head*
Lorz Italian (N. Italy)	*1 head*
Chef's Italian Red (Washington)	*1 head*
Purple Epicure (Mexico)	*12 cloves*
Spanish Roja (Spain)	*2 heads*
Creole Red (Louisiana, Mexico)	*2 heads*
Inchelium Red (Washington)	*3 heads*

They looked more like a selection of fruits than a selection of garlics. Fruits of different sizes, different colors.

The size of the full heads varied from that of a large golf ball (French Messadrone) to a large softball (Inchelium Red). And the color of the skins from a pale rose (Lorz Italian) to a dark red-brown (Spanish Roja); in between were white skins with stripes ranging from pale blue to purple, some of those with a red blush peeking through. Several of the loose cloves were as large as my thumb, some squat and blunt tipped, the size of a clove of California White garlic.

Feeling the body of the garlic heads with my fingertips, I estimated I'd be planting a total of approximately 140 cloves.

As I carefully laid out my new supply of garlics on the long dining table, identity cards under each variety, I knew they could not be planted in the earth alongside the cloves of California White that Dominic had given me. Not because there wasn't space for them, but because these noble aristocrats of the garlic kingdom deserved their own residence in a better part of town, separate from the living quarters of the hired help. All communication to such garlics would have to be addressed to the Royal Court, the two redwood boxes Robert and I would be building.

The sizes of the boxes had to be manageable, meaning not too expensive and not too wide, so I could easily reach the middle of the box from either side. They couldn't be too long, so we could wire the bottom before turning it over, and so the box would not break when turned. The ideal length: ten feet. The depth? Because gophers were unlikely to go over the top of a twelve-inch-high wall, we needed twelve-inch-wide boards. The ideal lumber was 2 X 12 redwood boards, ten feet long. Buying them fourteen feet long saved us a few bucks and also gave us enough lumber for the four-foot-long ends of the boxes.

Not only did I work hard, keeping up with Robert, I must have put at least six of the staples used to secure the chicken wire (half-inch mesh) through each finger.

By noon Wednesday the boxes were filled to their rims with soil trucked in from Santa Rosa. Sadie, rifle on her shoulder, steel helmet low over her eyes, patrolled one box and then the other. Now and then she stuck a probing paw into the soil, the way a person tests water with a toe.

Now and then she'd pause and sit, her tail curled around her. Woe to the first intruder, two or four footed, to show its hostile head.

Robert and I had become friends. Two years before, when I'd planted my first garlic crop (directly into the soil), he'd installed a drip system designed for eventual expansion. He must have sensed the inevitable.

Last year, when I'd planted the garlics he'd given me, he showed me how to add to the drip system already in place. It would be fairly easy, if not inexpensive, to extend the system to cover the two boxes, which would probably be as many as I'd ever need.

I'd paid for the materials and carried Robert's tools, but he wouldn't charge me for his time and talent. His only fee: an occasional dinner, plus the freedom afterward to surf the channels on my cable network. The Spartan members at the Farallones Institute considered television and DDT equally destructive pollutants.

For my own information and future independence, I helped Robert when he added enough tubing to the existing drip system to cover both new boxes. "We'll use rotary sprinklers for an hour today to get a quick, deep soaking. But before the soaking, I want to try a pH test."

"Why? What if I fail?"

"Not a test of you, a test of the soil."

"Why? What if it fails?"

He ignored me. Maybe he didn't hear me. In any event I lost nothing by letting him continue. I assumed that, as always, he knew what he was doing.

He brought a heavy toolbox and a long pack of plastic cups from his truck. A leather-covered kit the size of a cigar box came out of the tool box. He selected six cups, three of which (using a felt-tipped pen) he numbered 1, 2, and 3. Easy to follow so far.

On one of the three marked No.1, he wrote South end. On another: Center. On the third: North end. He placed the cups on the frame of box No.1 in their appropriate places. With a small tool the size of a tablespoon, he dug deep and brought up enough soil to almost fill each cup. After removing a container of sterile water from the tool box, he added enough to each cup to produce a muck the consistency of heavy cream.

"We wait an hour," he said.

In the house I began our supper. I also fixed a gin and tonic for both of us.

When we went outside at the end of the hour, Robert dipped separate strips of litmus paper (from the magic kit) into each cup's solution. Each strip of litmus paper, removed from its cup, was rinsed with sterile water. Its color was matched to a chart on which each of several colors represented a different pH level.

"Just about perfect," Robert said.

"My smart soil passed its exam?"

"With flying colors."

"Tell me about this hocus pocus."

Soil pH, Robert explained, stands for "potential of hydrogen," and is simply a measurement of the acidity or alkalinity of the soil. It is rated on a scale going from 0 (very acid) to 14.0 (very alkaline). The relative level considered neutral is 7.0.

Most plants, Robert went on, grow best when soil pH is between 5.5 and 7.0. A grower of most plants and vegetables has problems when the pH drops below 5.0 or goes above 7.0. At low pH (very acidic soil), plants have trouble absorbing important minerals such as phosphorus or potassium. Acid soil can destroy beneficial microorganisms.

"Garlic," he announced, quite pleased with himself, "likes soil around 6.8. Quite low acid, moderately alkaline. Almost but not quite neutral."

If my soil had been very alkaline, I would have had to bring it down toward neutral by adding soil sulfur and soaking it in for a few weeks before planting. That would have put off my planting for another month. I was already very near the late date. But I was okay. Rather, my soil was okay.

"Robert, all I want to do is grow garlic. Do I have to get a degree in chemistry to do that?"

"Nah. Most farmers didn't know about pH or even think about it. Especially the older growers—most of them gone now—from Europe."

"My father must have known."

"He knew but didn't know he knew."

"That's Poppa."

"You know Igor Yoshibofsky? From Graton? Old Igor doesn't know a damn thing about acid or alkaline or pH. But he can look at your field and tell you what's in your soil by the natural grasses or shrubs that grow there. Old-timers like Igor know these things because the lessons have come down over a thousand years of observation. If your soil's heavily acidic, you'll find weeds like sorrel or horsetail. Or ferns or blueberries. If you see true chamomile, field pepper grass, bladder campion, or goosefoot, your soil's heavily alkaline. Igor can tell you what to plow into your field when this or that grows there, so the soil will be better for growing vegetables the next season. He won't use the phrase 'correcting the soil pH.' He won't say anything. He just does it."

While we were eating our pasta, I remembered Dominic's concern at the sheep ranch when his vegetables were inexplicably small or wispy or tasteless.

"Who knows?" Robert said. "Maybe it's not a mystery. His soil's been used for a hundred years. In its natural state, before it was dug for the first garden, it was probably in ideal neutral condition. It could be tired now. You said he's constantly adding chicken manure. Maybe the manure is too hot, meaning too fresh. Maybe he's adding it too early. Or too late. The soil could be on fire with nitrogen. Who knows? He'd have to do a soil sample. Costs about a hundred bucks. Want to borrow my testing kit and at least check out his soil's pH?"

"He'd think I was a witch."

During the hour we'd waited before testing my soil's pH, we'd broken open the full heads of garlic and returned their cloves to their allotted paper bags, being careful to keep the identities of all varieties intact. The bags that had contained only cloves were placed in line with those bags of cloves we'd just separated.

After dinner, Robert said, "Now, while there's still enough light, I'll show you a neat little trick I picked up on the road to maturity."

He went to the truck and returned with an armful of newspapers. He selected enough to cover the soil from rim to rim in box No. 1. "About five pages thick," he pointed out. "Too few pages, too many pages, the paper defeats its purpose."

With a gentle spray from the hose, he soaked an entire issue each of the *San Francisco Chronicle* and the *New York Times.* "So the wind won't blow it around while we work."

"What's the purpose of the newspaper, Robert?"

As if searching for an answer, he dug about in his toolbox and produced a metal tape measure, with which he measured eight inches along the side wall of the box. He set a long nail in the rim, making sure it did not sink too deeply. He measured another eight inches along the other end wall of the box and set a second nail. He went on to set nails every eight inches around the entire perimeter of the box.

"Robert, what's with the newspapers?"

He held up a hand, signaling patience. Then, plunging his hand into the toolbox, he brought up a ball of yellow twine. After tying an end to one of the corner nails, he moved down the length and across the width of the box, producing, in four or five minutes, a grid of 130 yellow eight-inch squares.

"Why the newspaper, Robert?"

"We're talking literate garlic here, Chester. Garlic that needs to know what's happening in the world."

I waited. He was, as usual, marinating a batch of punch lines.

"Weeds," he said, "are the worst enemies of garlic. Call the weeds Nazis. Call the weeds the Ku Klux Klan."

"What the hell's the newspaper for, Robert?"

"Okay, if you insist. There are all kinds of fancy, very expensive materials out there to cover soil with, to smother the seeds of weeds. What's the cheapest? Paper. And, besides being much more manageable than the other materials, it also rots and goes back into the earth. Incidentally, before you ask, so you don't have to worry, lead's no longer used in commercial inks."

Back at the toolbox Robert produced a piece of iron bar about an inch thick and perhaps ten inches long. As he walked along one side of the box and then the other, he punched holes about three or four inches deep in the center of every reachable yellow-twined square.

"That's the advantage of a four-foot-wide box," he said. "Look, I'm short but I don't have to stretch to reach the middle."

Picking up the paper bag marked Inchelium Red, and starting at one end of the box, he dropped a clove—tip up, flat end down—into each hole until only two very small cloves remained in his hand. Those he returned to their bag. "Remember. Flat end of the clove down, pointed tip up. Tip about two inches below the surface of the soil. Got it?"

"Got it. Is the newspaper your idea, Robert?"

"No, no. Like all good ideas it was stolen from someone else. Now watch. I wipe the soil back into the holes so the clove's covered. I pack the soil down just a bit. Got it?"

"Got it."

From the toolbox: a fistful of long white plastic stakes. Robert printed on the broad head of one of them: Inchelium Red—Washington State—11/13/88—Box No. 1.

"Waterproof ink," he said. "So it won't smudge in the rains." He shoved the stake into the ground at the edge of the box until the identification data was about three inches above the soil.

As we moved from one variety to another, clove by clove, box No. 1 to box No. 2, Robert pointed out to me that where one variety ended and another began he was leaving a row of holes unplanted. For example: each row of Spanish Roja was eight inches from the next row. But Spanish Roja was separated from Creole Red by sixteen inches.

"Why do I do this, Chester?" He stretched a line of green plastic garden tape down the wide space and stapled it onto the rim of the box on both sides.

"To separate one variety from another, Robert."

"Go to the front of the line, Chester."

By six o'clock we had both boxes planted. Each variety, separated from the next, received its plastic identification tag (name of variety, country of origin, date it was planted, and the number of the box that was its residence).

"How many did we plant?" I asked.

"Let's see," he said. We counted the holes and compared our figures. A total of 139 cloves.

"In July or August," Robert said, "win or lose a few—weather, soil, cloves nicked or not healthy to begin with—you should have about 134 heads."

"Say I lose ten heads to...whatever. I'll harvest 124 heads. Say three heads to a pound. That's forty-one pounds. That doesn't count the California garlic from Dominic. Another twenty pounds. My God, what will

I do with sixty-one pounds of garlic?"

"Well, that's about a fifth of a pound a day. Fifth of a pound, that's about ten cloves a day. Easy. Or, you save a lot for planting stock next year. Want to build boxes for the California garlic?"

"That stays where it is. In the soil. We're not making boxes for that stuff. In fact, maybe I won't even grow it any more. I crave the exotic."

"Almost forgot something important," Robert said.

Again the toolbox. On a page torn from a notebook, he drew two rectangles. "The boxes," he said. He printed "1" in the corner of one box, "2" in the corner of the other. On the border of the page: an arrow, marked "N."

Each of the two boxes received divisions. Orienting the paper to match the direction the boxes were set (box No. 2 being the most northern), he printed inside each of the eleven divisions (six in box No. 1, five in box No. 2) the same pertinent details printed on the matching plastic stakes.

"A written record," he said. "You can make a neat copy in the house. This way you have everything recorded twice. In case the plastic stakes break or they're moved by heavy winds or storms."

"Or cats."

"Or raccoons."

"Or cats."

"Or crows."

"Or Sadie."

We unwound the yellow twine, pulled out the nails and hosed down the newspaper and garlic once more.

"Last secret," Robert said. "Come up to the truck."

In the truck bed was a half bale of straw.

"Straw, not hay. Cheaper. Fewer seeds. I use it as mulch."

In less than a half hour we had both boxes covered with a blanket of straw about six inches thick. Robert hosed it down so the winds wouldn't blow it away.

"I've never used mulch. What's it do?"

"It helps protect the garlic from frost in the winter. In the spring, it covers the young green tips, protects them from the birds. Crows and jays could nip off tips or even dig up the cloves. In hot, dry weather the straw gets soaked every time you water and it helps keep the soil moist underneath it. It can be a small pain in the ass in the spring because it germinates, sends up weeds. So you spend two, three hours a week, two or three weeks, pulling weeds. No big deal. After you harvest, the mulch can be plowed right back into the soil. Helps keep the soil loose."

I held up five leftover cloves too small to be planted. "These two are Spanish Roja, this one is Creole Red, these two are French Messadrone. This is my breakfast tomorrow."

After supper, while Robert watched TV, I tried to deal with my novel. Close to midnight, bleary eyed, I stumbled in from the study.

"You want to go home," I said, "so I'm going to bed."

"You've taken up too much of my time already," Robert said. He pointed to a page from his notebook he'd placed on the table. "Sometime before next summer I'll get a drip system in place for the garlic you're going to want to plant. I figure two or three more boxes. This is a list of the stuff you'll have to get. Harmony Farms is the best supplier."

"Who said I was going to build two more boxes?"

"I said two or three. You're too far in to back out now. You can only go forward."

I scanned the paper. It was a meaningless collection of abbreviations and measurements. "Is this a secret code for blowing up the world?"

"Pat, at Harmony Farm, will know what it means. By next year, when you expand, you'll be as familiar with drip irrigation as I am."

After he drove off and I started to turn out the lights I was suddenly aware of the dimension of the work I, we, had done these past two days. And I was curious about its cost. Not in energy or time spent, but in dollars and cents.

Why curious? Perhaps because I had been primed somewhere or sometime during the day when Robert had said "by next year when you expand...."

That was it!

Next year I'd be building two (three?) more boxes.

What the hell would I do with all that garlic?

I'd sell it. Then I'd build more boxes and plant more garlic and...ah! And make more money!

I'd been so sleepy a few minutes before, I could barely stand up—but now I was wide awake. I collected the pertinent papers and calculated.

Redwood: $68
Wire: $28
Staples: $3
Soil: $87

Total: $186. By the time I bought the drip materials, I would have spent well over $400.

I couldn't afford much more. After all, I'd soon be living on only my social security and my retirement.

Much more? What the hell *more* could there be?

Here I was, figuring how much space I'd need next year, when every clove I'd just planted would produce six to eight times as many cloves as I'd planted last year.

I'd need, let's see, I'd need about ten new boxes the year after next. That would mean five times the almost $400 I'd just spent for two boxes.

$2,000!

Forget it.

I decided to wait before telling Dominic Albini about my garlic. He'd have to see it and taste it to believe. That would be in about eight months.

I did not wait to call John Harris. "Garlic. New garlic. Get ready for garlic heaven. Passengers boarding now for Tochliavari, Georgia."

John called back two days later. "I got this weird message. You on something?"

"Rocambole," I said. "Spanish Roja. Creole Red. Russian Red Toch. Medidzhvari. French Messadrone. Tilth. pH."

"I better get some psychiatric medics up there. What's your address?"

"I haven't seen you for years, John. You haven't seen my new home."

"You've moved? Where to?"

"To Occidental. The garlic center of California, capital of the world! Gilroy? Where's Gilroy?"

"Chester, I can smell your breath from here."

Chapter 8

Maps? Journals? Pi-tooey!

My mother loved cats, but she accepted her husband's hatred of them. She permitted no cats in the house.

Her resistance to disappointments was always discreet, her rebellion against domination so creative as to often go unrecognized.

Almost always, when she crocheted doilies or tablecloths or coverlets or wall hangings—called *samplers* by pioneer Americans—she inserted in the most unlikely spots almost-invisible, often intentionally-camouflaged cats. Calicos, tabbies, shorthair, and longhair, they peeked from behind a vase filled with roses; they curled in a chair around a batch of multicolored kittens; or they stretched along a limb, all but lost in the midst of white or pink dogwood blossoms.

It's because of a cat that gophers now find it *almost* impossible to get to my garlic. One or two and then ten will someday find a way. And then? It will be total war!

I know they're down there, ready and waiting for me to make a mistake, which I sometimes do. (Once I put one-inch mesh wire on the floor of a box instead of half-inch; this caused the soil to build up around the sides of a box so that it became a gopher ladder. He just climbed over the edge and pulled down eighty-nine garlics in two hours.)

Since that day ten years ago when Robert designed and built my first two planter boxes, I've built thirty-eight more by myself.

Two of those were added simply to satisfy Oliveto restaurant's requests for spring garlic, which means the green leaves and the thin stalk along with the clove.

Spring garlic is generally plucked from the ground in early April. At that time, after six to seven months in the earth, the clove looks not much different from the day it was planted: a bit fatter, perhaps, and sporting long hairy roots.

Around late April or early May the clove spurts into growth, expanding and developing until, almost in a single month, it is a full head of four or six or eight or twelve cloves (depending on the variety planted).

Paul Bertoli, Oliveto's chef, remembered a spring garlic soup he'd been served in Italy. He has re-created it for Oliveto. It's hard to believe, but Paul's spring garlic soup is better than my mother's matzoh ball soup.

The two boxes constructed for the spring garlic are my final boxes. Forty is enough. More than enough.

Each year the construction of a single box exceeds by 20 percent the cost of construction a year earlier.

For the redwood required for those first two boxes in 1988, I'd spent $68. The wire, the staples, and the soil brought the total to $186, or $93 for one box.

The cost for one box the following year: $133.

Last year: $318.

Next year? The predicted increase in the cost of redwood alone is 30 to 40 percent.

At the moment, my inclination is to plant enough of my current varieties of garlic for Oliveto and for my own pleasure and health. Maybe I'll plant flowers in the other boxes. Or rye or wheat, so the deer can feast before they're run down by the neighbors' dogs.

Perhaps I'll grow hemlock for tea. Not for my neighbors' dogs but for my neighbors. Herb tea is very popular these days.

In addition to the cost of the construction of the boxes there are distracting pains: hammered fingers, stapled skin, smashed toes, singed rotator cuffs, festering sores from redwood splinters.

Being unwilling to ask Robert to help me each year, I've occasionally hired a neighbor kid. Each time, after he left, I had to put in another hour correcting his mistakes.

The job sounds simple.

Try it.

Especially try wrestling the roll of chicken wire by yourself. First: arranging the heavy boards into a "true" (ninety-degree angles at every corner) rectangle on a sloping meadow requires the patience of Job. Keeping them true while nailing them at all four corners requires the assistance of two of Job's sons.

Two or three men working the wire together simplifies the job. Working alone triples your exasperation. But using two or three helpers means paying two or three helpers.

I've settled on a system that satisfies me.

True builders would simplify it, I'm sure, but I'm not a builder by profession and, in trying to write, I discover I'm not even interested in truth.

I have no choice but to make the boxes exactly four feet wide, because half-inch galvanized-mesh chicken wire comes only in rolls four or six feet wide. So I have to buy the four-feet-wide rolls. Remember why? This is a test.

If I make the boxes six feet wide I can't reach across far enough, from either side of the box, to plant the garlic cloves in the middle region, or to weed the middle region. At harvest time, I'd have no choice but to climb into the box to pull the otherwise unreachable garlic.

On a box four feet wide, edge to edge, the wire, stretched tightly, barely covers the two-inch thickness of the side boards. No room for error. If there's even an eighth-of-an-inch gap, the gophers are up through the gaps and into the box.

So, I've finally learned to build a box without help.

I've designed a procedure for fixing the wire when I'm in the field alone, as follows. I staple the end of the wire at the two corners of one end of the box and walk the roll (which weighs slightly less than a baby elephant) the length of the box. When dropped, the roll serves as its own anchor, keeping the wire taut. I leave six inches of excess wire at both ends of the box.

Using wire pullers, I stretch out the wrinkles with one hand, while with the other hand I try to staple alternate corners.

In shifting and adjusting the wire with my fingers, I use the half-inch mesh for gripping. It's impossible to wear gloves. Cut and bloody finger tips are unavoidable.

I find it easier if I fix the wire tightly all around the box and then, after stapling the corners, I cut the roll free, remembering the extra six inches at both ends of the box.

Cutting the wire before fitting and stapling it in place is dangerous. The icepick-edged wire, springing free, can snap back, and the miniature icepicks can scalp you or blind you. Or both.

All this because I choose to work alone. Why do you choose to work alone, Chester? Because it saves me money.

Would Chester accept help? You bet he would, if it were free.

Appeal to friends, Chester. The job would be easier and friends, pleading for a day in the country, would expect no more than a good lunch. Right?

Wrong.

Chester has tried.

City friends who've offered help never arrive earlier than expected; in fact, they are almost always two or three hours late. What's two or three hours mean to dear old Chester? ("God, the traffic on the bridge was bumper to bumper. Sorry. You got something we can nibble on?")

Or they call at the time they've promised to be here to inform me they have to cancel. Baby has a boo boo on her tush; it could be leprosy. Or there's a concert at the New Fad Theater. "But hey, remember to save some garlic for us this summer. Love ya."

Now, when friends appear after the work is done, a sign designed by an artist in Sebastopol greets them where they park: THEM THAT WORKED, EAT.

Sadie must have been two or three when we met and she deigned to adopt me. That was my first winter in this house.

I'd arrived home from Saint Mary's College one night just before dark to find a gray mound on the front porch, sheltered by the overhang of the roof. What was I doing here? These were her quarters, but were I to ask politely, she might permit me passage. The decision would be hers.

I thought she'd run when she realized I was determined to simply pass her by. She growled, sounding like a pit bull.

Once I completed the gymnastics that permitted me to open the door without dropping my briefcase and books, the cat pivoted and demanded first entry into her house.

Following her directions, I built a fire in the iron stove.

I decided to give her a few minutes to dry herself and then I'd set her on her way.

Strong willed, I delayed for two hours the offer of a *small* bowl of warm cream. And…what the hell…that roasted chicken in the refrigerator surely would have been tossed in the garbage the next morning were it not eaten by someone this night.

I skinned and deboned the chicken and cut it into pieces suitable in size for a cat's teeth.

Since that night Sadie has not deserted or betrayed me.

In good weather (meaning anything but rain), Sadie lies on the deck or on the railing, alert (when she's awake) for the slightest hint of evidence of an impertinent gopher at work just below the surface of the soil: a quivering grass blade, a trembling plant leaf.

Three or four times a week, Sadie illustrates her good nature, performing her own little feline gesture of reciprocity: a gopher or two on my deck, at my front door. Three times, birds. Once a dead opossum.

I learned to avoid stepping out through the front door in the mornings in my bare feet.

Late one evening in February, soon after Sadie arrived, I pulled on my boots and my rain gear. Sadie, on the rug in front of the fire, watched my preparations as if she doubted my sanity. Given a choice of resting in front of the fire or going out in the rain, who in his or her right senses would chose the rain?

The path leading from the house to the two garlic boxes was a mix of weeds and rivulets of mud with, here and there, ankle-deep pools of water. The straw blanket on the boxes was compacted to no more than three inches.

I refused to even glance at Dominic's California garlic, since it was a full foot above ground. I had only soaked straw mulch, bare of even the slightest touch of green.

Then, as I approached the two boxes, my heart twisted in my chest. Three of the plastic identification markers in box No. 1 had been torn out of the soil. The blanket of straw mulch had been scattered. A few tips of severed green spears that had been concealed by the mulch lay like battle victims among the remnant strands of straw. One garlic clove was stretched out on top of the soaked newspaper, a victim gunned down in a desperate escape attempt.

Tending the wounded comrade, I lifted the clove and pushed it with great care back into the mud, scooping more mud to support it and covering it with handfuls of straw to keep it warm.

Unfortunately, I did not know which of my eleven garlics I had just tended. Without the plastic name tabs in place, it was impossible to know which varieties had been assaulted, which might now be lost, and which had survived.

The marauder could not have been Sadie. Refusing to go out in the storm for the last three days, she had taken advantage of the litter boxes in the house. It had to have been a raccoon or an opossum or another cat.

No matter. Guilt and revenge, at the moment, were the least of my concerns. With no identification markers I could not be sure, come harvest time, which garlic I'd be pulling out of the soil. I had not yet learned—by appearance, by size, or by taste—whether a garlic might be Spanish Roja or Creole Red or one of my other exotic varieties encased in the two boxes.

I'd betrayed my immigrant garlics, especially my Russian Red Toch. Those cloves were more than pieces of food, they were my friends, my family.

Then—"Aha!" I remembered the map.

The day that Robert and I had planted the garlics, he had drawn a map of each box. Then he'd drawn several rectangles inside the boxes, each a precise illustration of the location and name of each variety planted.

Most people who have gardens, small or large, resent the time and attention required to make such a map of their plantings. It is obsessive, it takes time, it dilutes the fun.

I resented it too. That's why I hadn't redrawn it, or placed it in the computer.

Now, where the hell were those two pages, the map explaining the pattern of my planting?

Devoted to garlic, it had no choice but to be in my garlic journal.

My garlic journal was designed, I'd promised myself, to contain all the details born of even the slightest experience with garlic. I've always kept a journal for the writing of my stories or novels (notes about people and places, words or phrases overheard). To make a map citing soil mix, source of fertilizer or mulch, source of garlic seed, was not a giant step. But I'd not thought about it since.

To supplement the map, as an instant reminder, I'd placed elongated white plastic stakes in the boxes, designating the site of each garlic variety. These stakes are always visible. Marked with waterproof ink, they can tell me, summer mornings or winter evenings, what is lying in this particular piece of soil. Should something—cat, dog, skunk, raccoon, wind, rain, awkward visitors—dislodge or destroy the plastic stakes, I had only my unreliable memory to save me. No, not true. I had the map.

But where had I put it?

Before I went inside I had a bit of repair work to do in the rain. Over the patches of bare, soaked soil, where the newspaper had been ripped away, I settled new pages from the *San Francisco Chronicle.* Over the paper I put as much scattered straw as I could collect. I gathered the six plastic stakes, hoping that in ten minutes or so I would return them to their proper position.

There was the journal. It was one of those lined notebooks that stenographers use.

Inside the journal was the map—two sheets of paper taped together at the middle, box No. 1 on one sheet, box No. 2 on the other. Before I left the house, I covered the map with Saran Wrap to protect it from the rain.

Back outside, in boots and rain gear again, I oriented the map so that the arrow designating west pointed toward the distant redwoods behind which, when the sun used to be in the vicinity, it always set.

With a wide space between each group of garlics, so there was no chance for one variety to slide over into the next, and with that wide space indicated on my map, the identification of the locations of each variety was simple. The plastic stakes were returned to their original sites.

After the damage was repaired, I had two cloves left over. They were forlorn, homeless. I pitied them. So, while standing there in the rain, I ate them.

Soaked, muddy, and exhausted, I returned to the front deck, where I dropped my boots and rain gear on the mat in front of the door. They could be cleaned and dried later in the evening.

The house was bitter cold.

First need: rebuild the fire.

Second, prepare a pot of water for pasta. Started immediately, the water would be boiling by the time I finished my shower.

After my shower I warmed four tablespoons of extra virgin olive oil, and added one tiny chip of a dried habanero pepper. After the pepper: nine or ten slices of reconstituted porcini mushrooms I'd collected the preceding November along the northern coast, near Salt Point.

The dried porcini were stored—dried in their own glass jar—on the shelf above my kitchen stove.

Other labels on other jars read: Boletus edulis—Porcini—collected and dried 11/11/86. Black Chanterelles—collected and dried 10/20/86. Candy Caps—collected and dried 10/10/86.

There, in the kitchen, stood my father. The mushrooms must have called him. We discussed the relative benefits of Russian Red Toch and the California garlics. Again: Pi-tooey!

My father was here in Occidental but he was also standing behind that splintered counter in the store in North Butler, Pennsylvania. The shelves behind him were empty.

Weren't the store's shelves always full when I was a child?

No.

Standing there, short, squat, dark, scowling, my father was writing numbers on a piece of paper.

"Boychik, I win the numbers tomorrow, the win it's five thousand dollars, I'll buy the old Willets farm. Chickens and eggs, I'll have chickens and eggs. You can't lose you raise and sell chickens and eggs. In this store God couldn't make a living. Pi-tooey!"

Poppa, you think you got troubles?

CHAPTER 9

This Ain't Garlic, This Is Cake

BY THE SECOND WEEK OF MARCH, the green heads in both boxes were an inch or more above the mulch, meaning that they were four or five inches above the soil, but those damn California White garlics of Dominic's were like miniature trees. My resentment toward that garlic was reaching dangerous dimensions.

Having been domesticated for fifty years, the California garlic should have been inferior to my garlics from Europe, which, for hundreds of centuries, had survived in their wild states through wars and plagues and other visitations from hell. I was tempted to simply stomp the California garlic back into the ground.

I didn't, of course. I had fond memories of my years of reliance on the stuff, before I'd met the new ancient garlics.

Was it possible that I had done something wrong? Had I killed the garlics David had sent me? Were they lying dead and deserted deep down inside the soil of boxes No. 1 and 2?

Then: *wham!* The gods gave me a sign.

In the section of box No. 2, identified by the plastic marker as French Messadrone country, were eight distinct green spears thrusting up through the mulch. I'd planted ten Messadrone cloves.

Four mornings later, in box No. 1, twelve Spanish Rojas. I'd planted two full heads, fourteen cloves. Not bad. Not bad at all.

By mid-March, boxes 1 and 2 were filled with green spears of various heights. Most of the varieties were returning the same number of stalks as cloves planted. None lost more than two. My guilt for having harbored doubts gave way to relief. I had not destroyed the garlics; I'd not betrayed David or Robert.

During frequent examinations over the next few months, I noticed the exceptional features of one or another of the varieties. Leaves varied from thin to broad, short to long; some leaves were thick and leathery, others as fine as grass; the angle at which the leaves left the main stalk varied (Russian Red Toch was more oblique, for example, than the angle of the French Messadrone leaves); some leaves stretched out like horizontal ropes, some reached out and up, like green candelabra; some of the stalks were thin, the size of a pencil, others were as thick as two or three pencils taped together. With appearances so different from the domesticated California garlic and, in fact, from each other, why shouldn't each of them offer a completely different taste?

Could the thin-stalked garlics be less healthy than the thick? Illness or disease can produce such symptoms in people or animals, why not in garlic?

Robert reminded me of what, of course, I knew to be true: Such variation is a common feature in all living things.

Still, we were very curious to find out if there would really be a wide span of taste among the various garlics, as David had promised.

What if these garlics *did* prove to be spectacular? Should I give them away? Eat them? Replant them?

Replant them? Why replant them? I already had more garlic than I could use in a year. In two years.

Like myself and Dominic, Robert had never eaten anything but California garlic. Until the exchanges with David at Seed Savers, neither he nor I had known that other varieties of garlic even existed.

Dominic still didn't know.

I'd never talked to any of the Albinis about my attempts to grow alien garlic, just as I'd never talked to other writers about my writing.

Whenever an old acquaintance from the Bay Area, a writer or college colleague, invited him-or herself up to my home for a visit, I limited the visit to an hour, all the while giving vague answers to the inevitable questions. About those two redwood boxes in the field: "Oh, I'm planting vegetables. I use a lot of vegetables." About my writing: "Oh, I'm plugging along. One page feeds into the next." About my living alone in the country: "Oh, you get used to it. I'm becoming more and more adept on the computer."

Left: Achatami, right: Acropolis.

Creole Reds

A partial collection of harvested and labeled garlics in my curing shed.

The last, a non sequitur, was also a lie. I was still basically a typist. My comfort with technology had ended when, at the age of nine, I tried unsuccessfully to use a Dick Tracy decoder ring I'd won in a box of breakfast cereal.

Once, at the Valley Ford ranch, Dominic asked how my garden in Occidental was doing. "Remember," I said "the only thing I plant these days is garlic." I went on and on about the promise the new crop showed. I could not bring myself to mention my European and Asian garlics.

I'd seen Dominic's garden at the Bodega ranch, of course. As had happened each of the previous 150 springs, that garden was alive and green. The perennial Albini crop of garlic, tomatoes, corn, peppers, and basilico looked pretty good. But there were patches where some of the vegetables, especially the garlic, seemed to be fading, seemed to be losing vitality. Perhaps next year, in passing, I'd just mention pH and sulfur.

"Did you plant any tomatoes or corn, Chester?"

"I've planted nothing but garlic, Dominic. I don't have a well that's reliable enough to plant corn."

"We'll have plenty. You need anything, come get it."

By late April both boxes were offering what I considered fully mature stalks.

What now?

Robert had general suggestions but, after all, he'd only ever planted California White garlic, and little enough of that. So, once again, I called David at Seed Savers. He was not available, but an assistant gave me advice.

"Now's the time," she said, after hearing my State of the Garlic Report. "Spray the leaves with a mix of Maxicrop and fish emulsion. Maxicrop is a collection of trace minerals. Fish emulsion is high in nitrogen. You can get both at a good nursery. Follow the directions on the labels. Spray the greens now, and in three or four weeks, spray again."

I was busily writing down her instructions and listening and trying to remember at the same time.

"For the next six weeks or so, the bulb needs help to expand. That's why you do foliar feeding. The clove absorbs the nutrients through its leaves. So spray now and then again in three or four weeks, and you'll harvest bigger and better bulbs."

On a Saturday in early May, preparing for the second spraying, I poked my finger into the soil of each box to check the moisture content. That was when I noticed strange stalks shooting up through the center of several of the varieties in both boxes. These, I concluded, were the famous scapes, announcing the fact that their classification was rocambole. Some of the scapes had already curled once and were moving into their second curl.

The eventual pod at the end of each scape was covered with a thin, light-green sheath. "If you don't cut the scape," Robert said, "that pod will open and you'll have a collection of little blue-green seeds called bulbils. Listen. That sound you hear is the pod of bulbils sucking energy right up out of the bulbs."

Following Robert's advice, I cut the scapes back as close to their juncture with the stalk as possible.

I convinced myself within forty-eight hours that the stalks were thicker and that the leaves, which had been limp, were greener and stronger.

Spanish Roja was the first of the garlics to go brown. That was near the end of the second week of June.

Several days later, the green leaves of the Creole Red meandered down the browning lane.

No more water!

Over a three-week period, the other garlics followed their leaders. I'd already memorized the general rule obeyed by thousands of small garlic growers like myself: when approximately half to three quarters of the leaves of any variety go brown, that garlic is due for harvest.

In the second week of June, the Spanish Roja satisfied that rule. I dug up every head.

Every five or six days, as the leaves of one or another variety died down, I dutifully and joyfully dug it up, being careful, as warned, not to cut a head with the tines of my spade. A cut garlic begins to degenerate immediately. If planted, its damaged cloves are susceptible to disease.

But my problems were only beginning.

Once pulled, the stalks and heads had to be cured. Cured where? And how?

I had no choice.

Each day saw more and more stalks of garlic spread across the floor of my house, until progress from living room to kitchen to bathroom became a virtual obstacle course.

I happened on a resolution to the problem when I visited some friends who had a baby. They lived deep in the redwoods near Camp Meeker, at the site of a sixties hippie commune. They had no laundry facilities in or near their home, which, smothered in fog and in eternal shade, was forever damp outside and in. Diapers, washed by hand, were hung near a brick fireplace inside the house, on a wooden drying rack bought at a local hardware store. Composed of horizontal dowels, the collapsible apparatus looked like a Tinker Toy project gone far beyond the inventor's intentions.

I bought two such racks at Occidental Hardware and set them up at the west end of my solar home, in the vicinity of my iron stove, which, of course, I was not currently using.

The Spanish Roja was the first to be pulled, on June 12; the last, Russian Red Toch, was pulled August 19. For no reason except balance, I tied the stalks of each separate variety in bunches of four or five and hung the bunches from the dowels, head down. Fixed securely to each clump was a tag containing facts about the garlic's identity.

By the end of August both clothing racks were filled to capacity.

To hell with the California garlic. It needed no such mothering. I left it outside, hanging, head down, from shaded tree limbs. It had proved to be as durable as I had thought, since it had survived defenseless against its enemies. But the gophers, roaming free in the unboxed earth, had depleted my supply to thirty stalks, now tied into six bunches.

September and October brought few friends. Not only was there no room in the house to entertain, but the aroma of garlic was so overpowering that several people who did appear at my front door went no farther. Approximately two hundred garlics expelling their moisture inside a small enclosure for more than a month can produce a unique and, to some visitors, very suspicious odor. I'm surprised no one reported me to local homicide investigators.

Two colleagues from Saint Mary's, who'd volunteered to help harvest but who arrived wearing white dresses, tactfully suggested we take our lunch on the deck. They stayed for an hour, then left to check out the shopping. I could have used their help hauling goat manure to my compost heap, but it might have ruined the polish on their nails.

By the end of the two-week curing process of the first garlics, I mulled over what to do with 175 stalks of garlic. They were still hanging from the dowels of their racks.

What I should do, I decided, is pay a visit to Maggie Klein at Oliveto in Oakland and to Alice Waters at Chez Panisse in Berkeley. Both women are close friends of John Meis, a former colleague of mine at Saint Mary's College.

I'd visited John whenever I visited Italy. He's lived in Tuscany for twenty-five years, and is a connoisseur of food and wines. He had recently published an informative and beautiful book called *A Taste of Tuscany*. In a letter to him I'd explained that my latest venture was growing new garlics. On a trip to Berkeley the spring before my harvest he had, in turn, informed Maggie and Alice about my eccentric experiments.

I called the restaurants, spoke to Maggie and Alice, and was invited to bring them samples, which I did.

Of course, I had to taste each variety after it cured that summer.

I ate each garlic raw, baked, on bruschetta, in sauces, in soups, and with meats. Even to my untrained and plebeian palate, the variations in taste were endless.

Trying to be scientific, Robert and I made notes about each variety as we chewed and inhaled. Sometimes we inhaled first, sometime we tasted first, and sometimes, we agreed, inhalation and taste raced to the finish line together.

I was amazed at how close—and sometimes identical—our reactions were. A few of the garlics were quite hot, a few quite mild; some had immediate and heavy impact of garlic taste, some had a thinner taste, with mild impact; the taste of some remained in the mouth for hours, in others the taste faded within minutes; some, we decided, could be better used in sauces, some in salsas, some on bruschetta. None so scalded the palate immediately and for as long as did the California garlic.

I set aside several heads from each variety for the fall planting. I would build however many boxes I had to. This was an indulgence I was willing to pay for.

So far I'd heard nothing from Waters or Klein.

I called Dominic and invited myself for supper, all of which, I insisted, I would bring. I don't believe he sensed an ulterior motive.

Having prepared everything before I left my house, I had the Albini's table covered with dishes of food in fifteen minutes. The pasta: plain old spaghetti. The sauce: fresh San Francisco Fog tomatoes stewed with rosemary (Dominic's) and twelve cloves of my Spanish Roja garlic. The dressing for the salad: extra virgin olive oil, balsamic vinegar, four crushed cloves of Achatami (from the Republic of Georgia) garlic. Slices of moderately toasted Pugliese bread (from a bakery in Sonoma), rubbed on both sides with Creole Red garlic and lightly coated with olive oil, salt, and pepper.

The raves began with the first bite of salad and crescendoed with the pasta. Even Brenda and Suzie and Robert, Suzie's husband, admitted that I'd somehow used the perfect amount of garlic. Their mouths weren't burning. Mary ate without comment but kept nodding her head, as if this were the correct answer to an unasked question. Marty and Dominic simply ate. And ate.

"That garlic," Dominic exclaimed. "The best yet. I've never tasted better garlic. I have to call my cousin. This is the best he ever gave me."

"Better not call him," I said. I excused myself and retrieved the paper bag I'd concealed in the kitchen when I'd arrived. I placed it on the table in front of Dominic.

Dominic removed the small carefully wrapped bundles from the bag and lined them up. He read aloud the words I'd written on the tape securing each of the six bundles. "Spanish Roja...Creole Red...Inch-In-Inchelemum Red?"

"Inchelium Red," I said. "The oldest garlic in America. Discovered on the Colville Indian reservation in Washington."

"All these are garlics? They all come from Washington?"

"They come from six different countries."

"Is this what you're growing in them boxes?"

"This is what I'm growing in the boxes."

"What about that garlic from my cousin's farm in Gilroy?"

"Oh, I have lots of it. I'll use it when my supply of this garlic is gone. These garlics don't last as long as the California White."

Dominic took a penknife from his pocket and cut the tape on the package marked Spanish Roja.

"Damn," he said, when he unfolded the paper and saw what he had. The head was larger than any garlic head he'd ever held in his hands, the cloves were almost as large as my nose, and the skins of every clove were dark red.

Dominic broke a clove free and started to carve the red skin away. Before he could apply his knife, the skin came off in his fingers. He grunted at the appearance of the large, creamy-white clove, and popped it between his teeth, onto the tip of his tongue. He appeared to be giving rapt attention to what was happening inside his mouth. He popped the skin of another clove and ate it.

"This," Dominic said, shaking his head, "this ain't garlic. This is cake."

When I returned home there was a message on my machine from Maggie Klein. "Chester, that garlic was divine. The chefs loved it. Especially the Spanish Roja and the Creole Red. They're beautiful, and the skin just rubs off. It saves so much time in the kitchen. And rich! I never knew garlic could taste so rich. More, more. Thank you so much. Call me. We are friends forever."

I went to bed with dreams of garlic dancing in my head.

The monies earned that year (1988) from the garlics planted the previous year (1987) came to $93.17. I can hear Dominic's cousin in Gilroy chortling. He spends more than that in one month for toilet paper.

Next year: ten more boxes. Well, maybe five.
Life was beginning again at sixty-five.
Or was it sixty-six?
No matter. Life, this garlic life, had arrived.

After the positive responses from Alice Waters and Maggie Klein to my first garlic offering, I'd planted representative cloves from the eleven varieties I then had and from ten varieties (from Filaree Farms, in Washington) I'd not planted before.

Ten varieties in 1989. Then, in 1990, twenty-two varieties. In 1994, thirty (thirty-two?) varieties.

Garlic from five countries, then ten, then fifteen.

At last count, seventeen countries.

Chez Panisse and Oliveto bought every extra pound of garlic in that first crop. They also offered to buy all the garlic I'd produce the following year.

Taking them at their word, I built ten more boxes, I brought in two tons of soil, and planted the second generation of my own garlics and bought others from Filaree Farm and Bob Elgard and Peaceful Valley.

In subsequent years I have bought garlics from these as well as other growers. Three or four times a year, friends, travelers, strangers, or anonymous contributors mail me packages of foreign garlics or drop them off on my deck or on the hood of my car.

Most of the garlics I grow now are hardneck garlics.

A subspecies of *Allium sativum*, the hardneck garlics retain much of the character of the ancient wild garlics. They are even called "wild garlics" by some growers. Unlike the stalks of California White, a softneck garlic, the leaves and stalks of the hardneck are so stiff and woody they cannot be easily braided.

Most of these exotic garlics do not survive as long on the shelf as does the California White. And so, around April or May, when my supply of my own garlics is depleted, I do as you do: I haunt the supermarket bins that are filled with Gilroy's California Early or California Late.

However, I am, and you must be, cautious.

The bins in those supermarkets are often filled with plump heads of blue or red-striped garlic. The price is double the price of the pure white garlic in the neighboring bins. The shopper assumes that the prettier and more expensive garlic must be superior. But in almost every case it is actually a sub-variety of the regular white garlic grown in Mexico or South America, where, news reports tell us, dangerous sprays are still the order of the day.

Do I buy this garlic? Only if the shop owner can verify that the garlic has been grown by one of those dedicated growers who has moved to Mexico to produce fruits and vegetables organically, without the use of pesticides. Growers, honest and dishonest, are attracted to Mexico because crops can be grown there for a fraction of what it costs to grow the same crop in the United States. When it's shipped here, the grower can double or triple his or her profits.

How to distinguish these concerned and honest growers from those intemperate growers who spread dangerous herbicides and insecticides on everything they touch?

You tell me.

Better yet, tell the Department of Agriculture.

Of my thirty (thirty-two?) varieties, I especially prize the following twelve:

1. **Mahogany** Deep-brown outer skin. Firm; good storing. Collected in the USSR in 1986. A good baking garlic. The raw taste flames down to taster's toes.

2. **Red Revel** Dark, brown red clove skin; firm bulbs. Originally collected in the USSR. After a long, slow bite: a good, rich taste.

3. **Purple Tip** Light-brown clove skin with splashes of bright red purple streaks. Top half nearly solid purple. Mild flavor. Originally from the USSR.

4. **Persian Star** Unusually vivid colors of clove skins. The bulbs have a sometimes smooth, white outer wrapper, but purple-streaked inner wrappers. The cloves have bright red tips and light streaks

on a whitish or yellow brown background. A very pleasant garlic flavor with a mild spicy zing. Purchased in a bazaar in Samarkand, Uzbekistan in the 1980s.

5. **Rosewood** Soft rose colors on large flat cloves. The cleaned bulbs are striking when large. Collected in the USSR.
6. **Shatili** Rose colored; can also have contrasting red purple streaks. Collected near the town of Shatili, Republic of Georgia. The taste starts sharp, drops off, then comes back nicely.
7. **Skuri** Striking clove colors, from rose to dark red and purple. Eight to twelve tall cloves to a bulb. The raw flavor is good, mild, and earthy. From the Republic of Georgia.
8. **Red Rezan** The bulbs are covered with a glazed purple blush. A strong and lasting flavor when raw, but not hot; no aftertaste. Collected near Rezan, south of Moscow.
9. **Redgrain** Not as much purple as others, slightly fewer cloves per bulb. Raw, not strong in taste, with a thick, grainy texture. Ideal for pesto. Collected near the town of Cichisdzhvari, Republic of Georgia.
10. **Georgian Crystal** Very large bulbs with four to seven cloves. A clean, white appearance, with beautiful fat cloves. Very mild when raw, but full of flavor. Also collected near Cichisdzhvari.
11. **Georgian Fire** Similar in size and appearance to Georgian Crystal, but averaging five to eight cloves. The raw taste is strong, with a noticeable but not unpleasant bite. A good salad or salsa garlic.
12. **Red Toch** Medium pink to light-red cloves. Very large bulbs. The raw taste is described as the perfect garlic flavor. Collected near the town of Tochliavari, Republic of Georgia.

Strange that all twelve are from the former Soviet Union, and that six of the twelve are from what is now called the Republic of Georgia. Would you believe that their presence is not by choice but by accident? Of course you wouldn't. There is no such thing as an accident.

Other growers, relatives, and friends have kept me going over the last eight years by sending me all these garlics without knowing a single detail about my father or grandfather. That he was from the former Soviet Union was one thing, that he was from Georgia was another. How did it happen then that almost half of my collection comes from the former Soviet Union, and half of that comes from what is now called the Republic of Georgia?

Tell me there is no such thing as fanatic genes destined to travel over space and time to guarantee continuity. Tell that to the Inchelium Red, which fed the Native Americans as well as the pioneers who displaced them. And which, after being forgotten for years, has been discovered again by a garlic lover/explorer on the Colville Indian reservation in Washington.

I stopped planting even a single clove of California White. Whenever my supply of exotic garlic was depleted, I borrowed whatever I needed from Dominic. I say *borrowed* because each year, as long as my garlics were available, I carried bags of one or another variety to him.

"More cake," he would say with each delivery. "Next time, how about some chocolate icing?"

CHAPTER 10

An Ancestral Aside

MY MOTHER WAS BORN IN POLAND. The lady—and she *was* a lady—was, as I grew up, so sensitive to the qualities that distinguish the decent life that I always have been and remain puzzled: How did a child of a Polish shtetl manage to become so gentle, so delicate, so beautiful, so refined, so humane?

She was only fifteen when she left Poland, not old enough to have had contacts with sophisticated cultural influences before she boarded the boat (and met my father, that Georgian anarchist) for America.

After she arrived in America, via Ellis Island, Johnstown (a sister already there), and finally Butler, Pennsylvania, who could possibly have introduced her to opera? Who could have taught her to tailor clothes and crochet? She spoke six languages: Polish, Russian, Hebrew, Yiddish, German, and English.

Ah, you say, I have no Polish garlic.

But I do:

Polish Carpathian Red From the Carpathian mountains of southeast Poland. Large uniform bulbs; not many doubled cloves. The bulb wrappers have a thin copper vein and variable purple blotching. Usually six to ten cloves per bulb. The plants are deep green and vigorous. A classic garlic flavor with a nice overall tang; hot, spicy, strong, and garlicky.

Polish Carpathian White The bulb wrappers are white. From the Carpathian Mountains in southeast Poland. Matures earlier than Carpathian Red. Hotter and spicier, with a stronger garlic flavor.

With garlic, as with everything else, my Momma was low keyed and discreet.

I wonder how my mother and father had behaved and what they'd talked about when they'd met at that Polish seaport. Did she consider him coarse? Did he consider her too aristocratic, too refined?

My father's image remains as persistent and firm at this moment as it had been when I was a child. As his voice and temper and bulk stood between my mother and me then, those qualities stand between her and me now.

It is almost impossible to see around my father's figure. It blots out foreground and background.

Is there any doubt about what I am trying to do with the growing of garlic and the parlaying of my dedication into a profitable business? How have I become what I am? What forces molded this professor/ writer/farmer?

A distant nephew of mine traveled to Georgia on a mission to unearth his roots. In a small village in what was still called Soviet Georgia, he discovered documents and photographs revealing birth dates, village names, arrival/departure dates of ships, hospital records, and naturalization papers. And a ragged, faded photograph of my father. Or a man who could have been my father's twin. Standing beside him was a younger man who, in turn, could have been *his* twin. On the back of the photograph, in ornate English script and beneath it in Georgian script, were the words *Tochliavari* and *Churin*. As a child I'd heard that last word. My father had once mentioned it as the origin of the name Aaron.

The photograph, a copy of the original, displays my grandfather standing next to my great-grandfather. Both men are wearing belted peasant blouses with tight collars banded with crocheted flowers. Both wear the classic Russian peaked cap.

My grandfather and great-grandfather were short and squat and very stocky, the older man's face abloom with the thick white beard of one of Tolstoy's peasants.

I'd heard dreadful stories about my father's childhood.

He stood in front of factories at the age of thirteen, handing out leaflets demanding rebellion against the Czar.

During a pogrom, one of a roving group of Cossacks had stormed into my father's cottage and, seeing my pregnant aunt, had ripped her abdomen open with a bayonet. My father grabbed a carving knife from a table and killed the Cossack.

Among my nephew's copied documents is a copy of a citizenship application; on the application a printed question ("Have you ever pledged allegiance to a foreign power?") and an answer written in the heavy, uncertain script I recognize ninety-one years later as my father's: "Yes, to Nicholas, Czar of all the Russias."

I'd seen the phrase in history books, but it had never had much impact. Seeing the words in my father's handwriting, I feel the sharp blade of an ancient and terrible history at my throat.

I have some of that crazy, courageous, savage, and perhaps self-destructive blood in my veins.

My father and I often strolled along the banks of the railroad tracks and the Connequenessing Creek in the fields and forests around North Butler, picking head-high elderberries. Or, deeper in the woods, we looked for dark-purple huckleberries and plump dewberries.

In October and November we gathered chestnuts, hazelnuts, butternuts, hickory nuts.

We waded in countless dawns through wet woods in search of mushrooms. I will never forget our rapture at the discovery of that thick red-orange rooster comb springing from the side of a decaying oak log. "Beefsteak," my father would sing. "Beefsteak! Beefsteak mushroom!"

How he enjoyed my botanist brother's reliance on ponderous Latin identification. "*Fistulina hepatica,* Poppa."

Poppa did not need my brother's scholarship to prove the mushroom's edibility. "And I never learned *Fistooluna hepypaty.* Ha ha!"

Indeed, inch-thick slices of the mushroom, oozing red juice, salted, peppered, and fried with garlic and onions, would surely be mistaken by the blind for prime fillet.

Here in California, every November (if October gives us adequate rain), I travel north on Highway 1, to Fort Ross, the old Russian coastal enclave.

In the vicinity of Salt Point, I park and walk the fields in search of what the old Italians, like Dominic, call the porcini mushroom. Adventurous beginners from the city call it the king bolete. My botanist brother (if he were alive) would call it *Boletus edulis*.

I watch as well for the porcini's equal: the *Amanita calyptroderma*, the coccora.

The coccora, which does not dry well, is best eaten very soon after picking. However, thanks to local Italians with whom I often scour the hills, I have learned how to store them. I clean several half-gallon milk containers, stuff them with my coccora, cover them with water, seal the containers tightly, and stack them in my freezer. I've thawed and used this edible *Amanita* four and five months after picking, and found the taste and consistency superb. The coccora is the main gem in my mushroom diadem.

Along with the blewitt. Latin name: *Clitocybe nuda*.

I eat this soon after gathering it, because it does not store well. However, here's a tip should someone favor you with a few pounds: slice it or cube it; fry it in butter on high heat for two or three minutes; turn the heat down and add, of course, garlic (a mild but tangy garlic like Purple Tip or Dukanskij); let cool and store no more than a month in a container in the freezer.

You've been over charged in restaurants for morels and chanterelles and porcini. Watch now as chefs pounce on the coccora and the blewitt. But keep a firm hand on your wallet.

I made plans last year to go to Georgia. Those plans required communication with the Russian Consulate in San Francisco. I called the number seven different times, and heard each time only a bored voice reciting in heavy Russian, and in an equally bored and heavily accented voice, a possible English translation. I chose all twelve options offered to me, leaving my phone number and address and the fact that, wanting to visit the Republic of Georgia, I would need a visa. What, I asked, might the next step be?

No one ever responded.

A librarian at the Santa Rosa library gave me the number of the Russian Consulate in Washington, D.C.

A message machine again. I left my number and the same message. No response.

After three more efforts over two more weeks without a response, I called the very helpful librarian in Santa Rosa again. She dug up the number for the consulate for the Republic of Georgia in Washington.

I dialed, and after three rings a human voice almost knocked me over. It said, I think, "Put on paper what want. Send paper Minister Agriculture, Republic Georgia. Address. Minister Agriculture, Embassy Republic Georgia, 1511 K Street NW 24, Washington, D.C. two zero zero zero hate."

There is and always has been a difference between Russians and Georgians, even when the Russians (for about seventy years) insisted that Georgia *was* Russia.

Having talked to several Georgians, and having read about my ancestral haven (or *one* of my ancestral havens, the other being Poland, whose consulate officials answer phones and write letters and manage, by comparison to their former so-called masters, to sound civilized), and having remembered my father, I can verify the fact that the Georgians could no more be Russians than ET could be Miss America.

The Russians are furious that for centuries, the Georgians have insisted on speaking a distinct Caucasian language, written in an alphabet of very elegant curving characters bearing no relation whatever to Latin or Cyrillic. It is a language and alphabet that the Russians found and find as un-Slavic as Mandarin Chinese.

Defense against never-ending conflicts is a way of life for most of the subgroups that make up the Georgian nation. The Savaneti people in the alpine region built famous watchtowers to guard against invaders. A tale from the nineteenth century relates that all of the inhabitants of the town of Ushguli shared equally in the execution of a would-be overlord by pulling together on a string attached to the trigger of a rifle pointed at his head.

Since before Christ, Georgia's fierce mountains have failed to protect it from scores of invaders—among them Mongols, Persians, and Ottoman Turks—all of whom broke the nation into fragments. Near the end of the eighteenth century, Georgia sought protection from Muslim enemies by turning to Russia. Not smart. In the early nineteenth century, Czar Alexander I, having put the nation of Georgia together again, gobbled it up.

After the Bolshevik Revolution in 1917, Lenin and the United States and Great Britain recognized Georgian independence. Four years later (surprise!) the Red Army invaded the republic and annexed it, and ever since Georgia has had to contend with contempt, hostility, and occasional insurrection.

Even today, Russia and Georgia really only have two things in common: the frontier that straddles the Caucasian Mountains between the Black and Caspian seas, and an obsessive love for garlic.

The country that gave me my father also gave the world Joseph Vissarionovich Stalin. Stalin came from Gori, a hundred kilometers south of my father's village. Tochliavari, near Vladikavkaz, hides in the forests on what had been the Soviet side of the Caucasian Mountains.

To the outside world Georgia is famous for its wines, but the one crop common to every ethnic/religious group—Georgian, Armenian, Muslim, Jew—is garlic. Each group speaks a different language, each group considers another group's garlic inferior, and each group sees as gold the specific garlic that has been passed down, literally clove by clove, from generation to generation, over a span of not years but centuries.

In the small villages, garlic is grown in plots sufficient to supply a family through nine or ten months of each year. There are fourteen different words for garlic in Georgia, depending on which village, or geographical or religious or political section you were born in.

The competition among village markets and in family gardens is almost warlike in its passion. There are as many varieties of garlic in the Republic of Georgia as there are family groups. Compare the Svaneti garlic to the Zemo to the Tochliavari to the Shvelisi to the Shatili to the Skuri to the Cichisdzhvari to the Machashi Chamiskuri to the Simunetti—all are small village gardens separated sometimes by less than a blade of grass, and often sustaining ten or twelve families.

The outer skins of a garlic grown thirty feet from another garlic possessed by another family, or clan of families, can vary in color from white to rose to dark red. The matured heads can be different sizes or shapes. One might be described as an Artichoke, another Porcelain, another Marbled or Purple Stripe.

Tamara Chaidze, approximately 102 years old, is almost as powerful as her namesake, Georgia's Queen Tamara, who lived in the late twelfth century. Tamara lives on the eastern edge of the village of Tochliavari, on the same road where, a kilometer to the south, a sawmill had been built fifty years earlier.

Since the disaster at Chernobyl, a thousand miles away in the Ukraine, the nearby lake and stream that once worked the sawmill have mysteriously dried up. Tamara's two eldest sons, who live at the foot of Mount Mkinvari (17,000 feet), no longer bring her mushrooms every two or three months. Along with herbs and berries, as well as deer and bear and rabbit, mushrooms remain so contaminated from the radiation fallout that the government has recommended complete abstinence from all such delicacies.

Tamara still lives in the same house where she was born. Each of her three husbands has added or removed one or another wall, raised or lowered the roof, planted a vineyard, uprooted the vineyard, planted fruit trees, replanted a vineyard, and replaced one or another chair or table or bed not because of style but because it had collapsed through years of use. Ten of her children, seven of whom are still alive, were born in this house.

A variety of documents stored in Tamara's cedar box, stacked with other ancestral icons beneath her narrow bed shaped from oak branches, indicate her birthdate to be 1894 or 1895 or 1896. A worn and faded religious text indicates that Tamara's mother was 104 years old when she died, and lists her daughter's birth date as 1893.

Her appearance belies her age. Her body is only slightly bent forward at the shoulders; her skin, though webbed with wrinkles, is brown and soft to the touch; her eyes are still lively and sparkling; her hair, gray but thick and heavy, is plaited and bound around and across her head—a style unchanged since she was a small girl.

Wearing an assemblage of cloths collected perhaps over a century, Tamara toils in the garden like a well fed, somewhat saintly troll. She has neither a bad word nor a bad thought for any living creature. She accepts without concern the tendency on the part of her children and grandchildren to join in the various battles that have embroiled her nation her entire life—up to the fall of communism and the subsequent growth of fierce factions destroying each other on the streets of large cities or in the fields and forests surrounding Tochliavari.

The civil war that has torn Georgia apart over the last five years has had little impact on Tamara's plot of land or the world of her mind. She lives her life now as she'd lived it seventy or eighty years ago. The regret she feels at the loss of her mushrooms is tempered by the fact that she still has her stock of garlic, the origins of which go back at least to the thirteenth century. Were it not for her ongoing crops of garlic, she would simply lie down beneath her quilts stuffed with goose feathers and silently wither away.

Tamara's five sons and two daughters, all in their seventies and eighties, have presented her with twenty-four grandchildren (now in their fifties and sixties), thirty-one great-grandchildren (now in their thirties and forties), fifty-two great-great-grandchildren (in their teens and twenties), and fifty-five great-great-great-grandchildren (babies). Two of her sons are in their twenties, born when she was close to eighty.

These sons, using horse-drawn carts, bring their mother firewood and pelts of fox, wolf, bear, and rabbit, which Tamara cures and sews into garments for the harsh winters.

But Tamara, practically a republic unto herself, is not, in Georgia, that unusual.

In Tochliavari alone (approximate population 312), there are eleven people in their late nineties or older. Most of them, like Tamara, dig up their own garlic late every summer, and immediately hang the stalks under the thatched roofs of ancient barns. (The roofs of more contemporary barns are covered with tar paper, which radiates heat and ruins garlic.)

Tamara has seen so much of life that she is prepared for death, which, to her, will be a simple and routine change of residence.

Each day, using what might be termed a pitchfork (an oak pole tightly fitted with three pointed stubs from a beech root), Tamara turns the soil in her garden, or transfers piles of hay and manure (goat and cow and horse, cured now after a season under tattered patches of plastic gathered by sons and grandsons along the roadways or riversides or train tracks) to the potato and tomato and pepper plants, and, of course, to her treasured garlic.

Every Saturday afternoon, she selects a fat goose or chicken for the Sunday night supper, attended by the two sons who live near Mt. Mkinvari. At the rear of the house, at the same stump her mother had used for the same purpose, she swings the goose or chicken in swift circles to daze it, and then lays it in place and chops its head off with one quick blow from the same scarred hatchet her mother had used. Two pigs come running from the roadside ditches to fight over the blood-soaked, feather-strewn muck that now surrounds the stump.

In the autumn, in jars accumulated over the last fifty years, Tamara preserves a variety of fruits and vegetables and, when she's fortunate, venison. In the same dark chamber that contains her jars, two earthenware crocks are forever filled with her lifeblood: yogurt. Georgian lifeblood.

Tamara Chaidze, as did her ancestors, and as do her countless progeny, attributes her long life, vigor, and remarkable health to a drink that has long been a staple in most of Georgia, as well as neighboring Armenia and parts of Afghanistan and Azerbaijan.

The drink, garlic wine, varies slightly from village to village, and from family to family, depending only on the garlic used.

Two large mugs of garlic wine are to be drunk first thing in the morning, again at bedtime, and eight or ten times in between. The recipe is simple. All the ingredients are grown or produced in the garden or in pots in the kitchen, in every house in Tochliavari. In the capital city of Tibilisi, garlic wine can be purchased in every market. It is the only drink that competes with the world-famous Georgian wines made from the Georgian grapes.

Garlic Wine

Fill your mug with fresh goat yogurt. Add as many crushed cloves of Red Toch garlic as you wish, but no less than four. Stir. Add ten to fifteen leaves of mint, sliced into small strips. Let sit for ten minutes. Drink slowly.

On those rare occasions when Tamara feels weak or ill, she drinks her garlic wine every hour. If her supply is near depletion, someone is sure to bring her several jugs of yogurt or wine from their own storerooms.

Each family has its own herd of goats, but they all use the starter, called the *matushka* (the Russian term for *mother*) passed down through countless generations. It is only certain that the original was a gift from God, the mother of us all.

When asked how she has managed to bury three husbands, who had also relied on garlic wine but who died in their fifties, Tamara shrugs and points somewhere within the layers of cloth where her lower abdomen might reside. "You enjoy a man as long as he's here and when he's worn out you get another one. Like a cow."

Chapter 11

The King, Again, and a Visit from Momma

I was still asleep when the garlic king called.

He feigned self-reproach. "Did I wake you up? I always do this. Wake friends up. But you're retired. You can sleep whenever you feel like it, anyway. Or write. Are you writing?"

"Sometimes I work all day and sleep all night, sometimes I write all night and sleep all day. Sometimes I fly to Cleveland."

"But you are writing?"

"Mostly, the last two months, I've just been working outside. How are you? Where have you been? You were going to come up here—when? A year ago? Two years ago? I've thought about you. You got me into this, you bastard."

"This? What the hell is *this?*"

"Garlic."

"I ran into Maggie Klein at Oliveto and she tells me you sold her some rare and exquisite garlic last year and they expect ten times as much from you this year. Rare garlic? Exotic garlic? Incredible garlic?"

"Right. I'm growing rareexoticincredible garlic. Currently thirty varieties—I don't know yet if I have thirty-two—from about twenty different countries. Last year, for the first time, I sold some of it. To both Oliveto and Chez Panisse. The chefs at both restaurants liked it. Raved, in fact. So I expanded my production for this year."

"Thirty varieties? What the hell does that mean? And what's this cockamamie 'I-don't-know-yet-if-I-have-thirty-two?'"

"Well, I have two mystery garlics. I don't know if either one will grow here in Occidental. I won't tell you where they're from. I've been nursing them for two years. Very exotic. Underline the *very.*"

"Chester, you're beyond cool. How would you like to be the star of a garlic festival? Of my, our, garlic festival? *Our* meaning Oliveto. I'm organizing it for Maggie."

"No, thanks."

"You'd be famous."

"Selling garlic?"

"Oliveto hired me to promote a week-long garlic festival the third week in July. I've brought in two women to do PR, and they're getting a press release together. Maggie and Robert want to use your garlic. Every piece of paper that goes out of the restaurant will refer to the fact that only the garlic from Chester Aaron's farm in Occidental will be used throughout the festival. How about it? The PR women and I want to visit you, see what you're doing. We'll take pictures. We'll work in the fields. You probably need help harvesting. How about it?"

I knew I should have said no, but the idea was tempting. My investment in garlic (physical, emotional, spiritual, financial) was suddenly being offered legitimacy.

"Look at it this way, Chester: you'll be building an audience for your writing. A writer, professor, farmer. And you're sixty-nine, for Christ's sake. I'm on my way. With Denisen Eleanor."

"Who's Denisen Eleanor?"

"Denise *and* Eleanor. The PR twins."

"John, I have to start making some money on my garlic. At least enough to pay expenses…"

"The festival will do that. I promise. Give me directions."

With the arrival of John and Denisen Eleanor I discovered that a news release about the garlic festival had gone out a week before. We argued about their having set dates before talking to me. Setting it in the month of July could make it difficult. I don't harvest many of the garlics until June or July. And after harvest, the garlics should cure for two or three weeks to eliminate water and to develop their unique flavors.

But neither the dates for the festival nor the tasting could be changed.

I had my first of many chills. "Tasting?"

"The first official garlic taste-off in history."

"You haven't even tasted my garlics yet."

"Doesn't matter. I trust Maggie Klein and I trust you."

"How's it work? What do we do? What do I do?"

"We'll figure that out. Just trust me."

"Us." Denisen Eleanor chimed in from the depths of the house.

I would be interviewed by Denisen Eleanor, and a copy of the interview would be sent to the food editor at the *San Francisco Chronicle*. The editor's full-page article (already promised) on garlic would inform the public five days before the garlic festival began. Other editors and reporters and food writers from the Bay Area, as well as Los Angeles, were still being lined up. The *New York Times* and *Gourmet* magazine had promised to send stringers. *Sunset* magazine had expressed interest in doing an article about garlic in general and Chester Aaron and his garlics in particular. Chefs from the hottest cafes and restaurants in California would be in attendance. For the entire week, Oliveto would be offering special garlic-infused lunches and dinners.

"A happening," John promised. "Stalls. Balloons. Music. Free samples. A children's tasting. Serious gourmet dinners with Gold Medal wines. Special *name* customers who dine regularly at Oliveto are being invited as guests. I got permission to show Les Blank's film *Garlic Is as Good as Ten Mothers*."

Did I have a vita I could send Denisen Eleanor?

Did I have any photographs?

Would I be available for interviews by writers from national magazines who might want to drive up to Sonoma County to visit me?

"God, I'll go to my grave famous for my garlic. No one will remember my novels. Remember, John, I'm really up here to write, Goddamn it."

"But you obviously want to grow garlic, too."

"I obviously do."

Denisen Eleanor wondered why I had to choose.

"Well, I don't think I can do justice to both."

Denisen Eleanor's response was simple. "Then choose one and give up the other."

Denisen Eleanor can't understand, because they're only forty years old. Children.

"Write about it," John said.

"Write about it. Sounds so easy. Why didn't I think of that?"

"I remember you telling me once," John said, "that a writer wastes nothing. In the kitchen the chef wastes nothing. You're writing and you're growing garlic and, if I know you, you're cooking with garlic. Write about growing and cooking with garlic."

After John and Denisen Eleanor left that evening I sat at my Mac Classic and inserted a new disc and gave it a title. *Garlic.*

I studied the word, deleted it, and gave it a different title. *A Garlic Life.*

The phone rang. Edwin Honig was calling from Providence, Rhode Island. He was going to be in Berkeley for two weeks. We should meet.

We should and would.

Edwin, a poet and translator and critic and professor, had lived with his wife and two children on Dominic Albini's sheep ranch in Bodega before I'd lived there. They'd turned it over to me. He and I have remained close friends.

I told Edwin I had, just before he called, begun a new book.

"What's it about?"

"It's about garlic. Me and garlic. My life and garlic. Folklore and garlic. Garlic and politics."

"Sounds like a crazy book. What's the title?"

"A Garlic Life."

"How about placing an *Oh* and a *this* in front?"

"An *O* ? The letter *O ?*"

"An *O* and an *H* and a comma. So it would read, *'Oh, This Garlic Life.'* In English and Spanish and Portuguese—and I speak as a poet now—that *Oh,* separated by a comma from the next three words, forces a pause that is reverential. It says 'This wonderful, magnificent, totally satisfying life that is defined by the mysterious herb garlic.' It is an herb, isn't it?"

After our promise to meet in Berkeley I turned to my Mac and changed the title as he had suggested.

In the middle of the night, I woke up and went downstairs to my computer again. In the last ten years, garlic had given me a new life.

I erased *Oh, This Garlic Life* and replaced it with *Garlic Is Life.*

A monstrous dream invaded my sleep. My delicate mystery garlics were being consumed by a giant gopher wearing a Russian Cossack's uniform. Sadie was serenading them on her balalaika.

I woke up, perspiring. Dressed and carrying a flashlight, I walked down into the field to check box No. 13.

My two secret-exotic-mysterious-rare garlics did not as much as show a hint of green above the mulch.

On the way into the house, I took a detour to my curing shed, which I had built right after the second year of curing the garlic in my house. I'd had to build it because by then I'd expanded to the use of not two but five collapsible laundry-drying racks. I was having trouble finding space for my toothbrush.

The curing shed had cost me five thousand dollars. I took out a Wells Fargo equity loan to pay for it. So? As my father would say: "Pi-tooey! So do it, already."

The shed, constructed of redwood, has fans to cool the garlic during extremely hot days. One fan also sucks out the humidity on damp days. There are two stories. On the first floor, sixty wires are strung wall-to-wall, six levels high. Those wires are capable of holding four thousand stalks of garlic—more than half a ton.

The loft is used as storage and curing space for my French Red shallots, which I'd searched out at the request of a friend who is a chef in San Francisco. In checking catalogues for exotic shallots, I had discovered Le Jardin du Gourmet in Vermont. They offered three different shallots: French Red, French Frogleg, and French Gray.

The first year, I ordered five pounds of the French Red. The response was so positive, I ordered fifteen pounds the following year. Fifteen pounds of seed gave me seventy pounds at harvest time.

Then I was foolish enough to give a pound of free samples (enough for about ten meals, at fifty bucks a meal) to the owner/chef at a four-star restaurant in Berkeley.

National and international publicity for the restaurant assures the dining world that this person scours the farmer's markets for the very best meat and produce. Price matters not at all.

She loved them. Exactly, she gushed, as she remembered them from Paris.

But in the end, she made no offer to pay for the shallots I'd given her. She did not offer me a free meal. She did not say, "Thank you, Chester, for the freebie shallots." And she did not say, "We want to buy more of these shallots."

The same chef had once raved about my garlic, after tasting a free sample of it. She said she'd tell her patrons that the special garlics came from Chester Aaron, who lived in Occidental, in Sonoma County. "Thirty pounds a week," she said, "no matter the price. They're organic, they're new, they're delicious." After I delivered the garlic and the invoice, I received a call from the chef. "Hey," she said, "I can buy regular garlic at the store for half the price you're asking."

"Go buy it," I said.

I sent her a clove of my hottest Mexican garlic for use as a suppository.

Should I buy, I asked myself as I walked to my curing shed, that new garlic I'd seen advertised in the recent catalog from Filaree Farm? It was called Leningrad. It was $28 a pound, *if* Ron Engeland still had any for sale.

Leningrad, Filaree's catalog informed me, grows tall, sometimes up to four feet. The Porcelain bulb wrappers are tight, white, highly symmetrical, clean looking, and paper smooth. The background color is a shiny brown. If a blush does appear on part of a clove, it is a brighter red than the red that occurs in the rocamboles. This particular garlic was collected near Leningrad, in the western republic of Russia, near Estonia.

Should I?

My checkbook's current balance was around $150.

Leningrad. It was not Georgian, but how could I resist?

Poppa was there in the air before me as I approached the curing shed. He was dancing the *kazatsky*.

Inside the shed I reviewed the empty lines. All the garlics that had hung here after last year's harvest were long gone. Sold to Oliveto or sent to friends. In three months these now-empty lines would be heavy with just-harvested garlic.

I turned off the light, but before the glare faded I knew there had been an apparition. Someone had been standing there in the break between light and darkness.

Is that you, Momma? Why now?

Ah, yes. My consideration of the Leningrad garlic.

Think, Chester. Didn't you notice another, different garlic in Filaree's catalogue? A garlic from Poland?

I returned to the house, very hungry. But first things first.

I opened the catalogue. There it was. "A new and lovely Polish Carpathian White. Replacement for the previous white. $21 a pound."

Was that a smile on my mother's face? Was that a scowl on my father's face?

New and lovely. That had to be my Momma.

Do it!

Next October I'd plant the new (and lovely) Polish Carpathian White in the same box as my fierce Russian Red Toch.

My mother also loved fruit, especially apples, pears, and cherries.

My first January in Occidental I purchased so many bareroot trees I lost count. They went into the earth on the opposite side of the road from the house. That was ten years ago.

All the trees were encased in wire cages that I constructed from a roll of chicken wire. I learned how to cut and shape the wire so that the roots inside the cage went down deep. Once the hole was filled, a three-inch collar of wire rose above the soil. That would keep the gophers, frustrated at their inability to get at the roots, from going down to the roots from the surface.

Each of the fifty fruit trees I planted that year, and the next, has survived.

In the spring and summer, a profusion of blossoms attracts birds and bees and friends from short and long distances.

In the last three years, during the summer and fall, as the fruits ripened, Robert and Nancy Salz brought their children, Caroline and Hadley, and Hadley's friend, Claudia, and from those visits I won pints and quarts of jams and preserves, and pies.

I thought of my mother during those days. She would have sat in the shade on the deck, crocheting an image of a comice pear or a platter of bing cherries (with a cat hidden in there somewhere), smiling, humming.

When the visitors are my own son Louis, and his wife, Susan, and my grandchildren, it's almost too easy to make the decision that this life of mine has been worth the struggle and heartache.

I do not have a single thing to complain about.

But why not keep trying?

CHAPTER 12

Conference Call, Big Time

TWO DAYS AFTER THE VISIT BY JOHN and Denisen Eleanor, Sadie and I were making our way through our suppers when the phone rang.

Did I have a few minutes? Would I participate in a conference call?

"Conference call? Is this Wall Street?" Denisen Eleanor were at John's house, in his office. "We have to talk."

Could I, Denisen Eleanor asked, supply them with some information about my life, about the reasons for my obsession with garlic, about how the various garlics are different from each other, about how to distinguish best garlic from very good from lousy? Did my exotic varieties require special treatment? Given the fact that they were not native, and given our ongoing drought, had they, transplanted from foreign soil and foreign climes, suffered culture shock in Occidental, California? If my garlics were so superior, could I explain why Gilroy doesn't grow them?

"Okay, first, why Gilroy doesn't grow them. My garlic requires such constant personal attention that Gilroy could not afford to grow it. They're automated. They've spent many years developing a perfect soil for one perfect product and a perfect marketing technique for that single product. To change to production of my kind of garlics they'd have to develop a new production technique, new marketing techniques. It's like Ford or GM having to retool to reproduce the Rolls-Royce line and then convince the world their product is even better than the original. For the new garlics they'd have to charge three times what they charge for their white garlic. Result: tradition-bound consumers would rebel. Millions would be lost. Dollars, not garlics. The market for my garlics remains insignificant by Gilroy standards."

"Do you have much help, Chester? We've seen your place. There's so much work."

"I do most of the work myself. When I'm a few bucks in the clear I hire a few kids to help. I rely on Robert Kourik for occasional help and frequent advice."

"Kourik. He writes gardening books." This from Denisen Eleanor.

"That's like saying Hemingway only wrote stories. Robert writes about the land and the water, and the use of gray water, and the use of drip irrigation. Robert's an experienced gardener, a publisher, a freelance writer, a consultant on gardening."

"Okay. So you use drip irrigation. And Chester, would you talk slowly, please. I'm taking notes."

"Robert helped me set up my irrigation system. When he talks or writes about food, garlic, radicchio, or lavender, he considers its journey from seed to mouth to toilet bowl and how that journey fits into the earth's design. If I didn't use his drip system, I'd be wasting a lot of the precious water my well manages to cough up. Robert's so far ahead of most of the so-called garden experts, he's in a league of his own. The trouble is, he's very eccentric. He takes no shit from anyone; he writes and says what he thinks. For that he's avoided by the experts who pontificate in newspaper columns for earth-firsties dressed in Smith & Hawken gardening clothes that cost more than my mortgage payments."

Denisen Eleanor: "That takes care of the water questions we won't ask again thank-you very much. Honestly—and please, no lectures—doesn't soil and weather vary from France to Italy to Russia to California? Those garlics that come from other countries might not grow well here. Right? We have to know these things in case some reporter asks us a question tomorrow or the next day."

"You're right. Soil varies. Not just from country to country but state to state, county to county, farm to farm. From one of my boxes to the next box. I buy and build and mix my own soil. If, in three years, a garlic doesn't adapt to my soil and my weather, it's replaced. Given the weather in Occidental..."

Denisen Eleanor: "Wait, wait. Don't talk so damn fast. Given the weather in Occidental..."

"...It's unlikely that I'm going to have luck with a garlic from the frozen tundra of Siberia or the deserts of Israel. John, is it possible to have more time?"

"I thought we settled this the other day."

"We did. But farming is unpredictable. In January ask any farmer in the Midwest what day in September he plans to cut the wheat or pick his corn. Ask any owner of any vineyard in March what day in October he's going to pick his grapes. All sorts of things can happen."

"Like?"

I decide against the tip-of-the-tongue response that speaks to genus and species and variety, *Allium longicuspis* (wild species) versus *Allium sativum* (domesticated species), essentials of soil nutrients, choices of fertilizers and a dozen other potential themes.

"I grow varieties of garlic from a variety of countries. I'm a beginner. I never thought about the possibility that what grows well in New England might not grow well in California. Will big, beautiful red-skinned bulbs from the former Soviet Union shrink to pale plum-sized heads here in Occidental? Too much rain, too little? Cow manure versus chicken manure, good drainage versus poor drainage? Gophers? Everything affects everything. The little wheels move the big wheel. The wristbone's connected to the skull bone."

Denisen Eleanor: "Slower, Chester, slower."

"I won't know how good the garlic will be until I actually pull it out of the ground. Example: I have a garlic called Medidzhvari. The heads last season were small. The same garlic in its native Georgia produces large heads. In Georgia this garlic is extremely hot; here my Medidzhvari was only moderately hot last year. Was that a function of the fact that a Soviet peasant might have used human shit as fertilizer? A function of annual rainfall? A function of...you fill in the blanks."

Denisen Eleanor: "We can't use all of that with the reporters, I guess. Okay, why are you so worried about the dates we've set?"

"What if it rains right up to the day of the tasting and the garlic I've promised you isn't dry enough to be pulled, which means its curing process will be delayed? Fresh, wet garlic is not half as tasty as cured garlic. The tastes that distinguish one variety from another will not have settled. They'll be diluted. All garlics at that stage tend to taste alike. What am I to say when your experts whine, 'But this poo-poo garlic doesn't taste any different from that pee-pee garlic?'"

Denisen Eleanor: "All dates are set, Chester."

Two PR packets, I am told, describing the festival and the tasting, have already gone out to chefs and food writers, local and national, to newspapers and radio and TV. Several people have already phoned to say they've arranged their travel schedules to include the garlic festival.

"What," I ask, "is the official and final date?"

"July 24 to 31," John says. "So we won't compete with Chez Panisse's annual Bastille Day dinner. The 24th starts it off with the Tasting."

I hear Denisen Eleanor groaning all through my next response.

"The third week of July could mean the best garlics might not be harvested. It would be like eating unripe apples. An unripe Jonathan tastes just like an unripe Arkansas Black or an unripe Fameuse."

"Okay," John said. "Go on." (As if I'd not intended to!)

"The taste unique to each apple, the taste that distinguishes a Fameuse from a Red Spitzenberg, heightens only as each apple, in its own genetically unique calendar, reaches its sugar peak. Once it's sugared, a bite of each, even with your eyes closed, *especially* with your eyes closed (so you cannot cheat by relying on shape of fruit or color of pulp), will tell you without fail which variety you're tasting."

Repeated to me for the fourth time: plans were too far along to permit a change of dates; important participants had already been informed and had set their schedules; writers such as Sibella Kraus from the *San Francisco Chronicle* and Michele Anna Jordan from Sonoma County's *The Paper* and Paula Hamilton from the *Oakland Tribune* and Lauren Swezey from *Sunset* magazine—none of them would be able to alter their fixed schedules. "These are important people, Chester. Important for the restaurant, important for your garlic, important for you."

I knew, of course, I had no choice. They had a job to do. Well, in for a dime, in for a dollar.

"Okay," I said, "I promise to have five to ten pounds of at least ten varieties of garlic from maybe five countries in the chefs' hands ten days before the day of the tasting. So he can test each variety. If we're lucky, I could have maybe twelve or thirteen varieties from six or seven countries."

Those garlics, if the gods of garlic smiled, had to be ready for harvest at least two weeks before their delivery date. That would mean harvesting in mid-June. That mid-June harvest date would mean withholding water from late May on, so the heads would have three to four weeks to fully form and harden and begin to dry off.

Denisen Eleanor: "What if it rains in May, as it usually does?"

"If it rains hard and long, everything will be set back at least a month."

It so happened that the garlic gods heard my prayers, and even apparently respected them. There was not a drop of rain after May 12. Three, four, five times a day, I checked weather reports in newspapers and on the weather channel. No rain in the forecast. Which meant it would almost surely rain.

I examined every redwood box every morning. Each day in one or another box the green leaves on the garlic stalks moved into varying stages of drying down, meaning turning brown.

Two boxes of Spanish Roja, which had been planted on September 27 of the preceding year, 1992, were the first to be tested.

Digging carefully, so the tines of my spade would not cut the garlic or tear the bottom wire on the box, I lifted out the first row of nine heads of Spanish Roja.

Perfect.

I mean *perfect!*

The heads were larger than my fist; each clove was the size of my nose; a very small portion of the outer sheath covering one clove of one head, tenderly pulled back, disclosed a bright red, almost-vermilion skin covering the white meat.

I harvested the garlic from those two boxes, tying three or four stalks together in single bunches.

The two boxes supplied thirty-five bunches. I fixed a tag to each bunch: Spanish Roja, solarized, in 9/28/92, out 6/10/93.

Solarized means that the soil in that box had been soaked immediately after the garlic was pulled the previous year and after the soil had received an abundance of aged manure and my own aged compost. The box was then covered with white plastic, which was stapled as tightly as possible to the sides and ends of the box.

The soil beneath the plastic then steamed for two months.

In theory, all the seeds, bacteria, and possibly dangerous meanies that could endanger the next garlic crop would be killed, but only to a depth of about ten inches. That would allow my wise earthworms to burrow deeper in search of a cooler sanctuary and survive there.

A scan of my 1992 journal relating to planting informed me that box No. 1 had had a hundred pounds of aged chicken manure added in 6/5/92, and had been double dug and then solarized from 6/8/92 until 9/27/92, at which time I'd removed the plastic cover and planted the cloves.

The phrase *my seed* means that the cloves had come from my own crop of the year before (1991), not cloves purchased from Filaree Farm or from Bob Elk Elgard or from Pleasant Valley Farms. The two mystery garlics, gifts from friends who'd returned from Europe, were still mysteries. In one more year, the mysteries would be solved.

Robert Kourik had expressed his doubts about solarizing, suggesting that, given the work and time and expense involved, the benefits (considering the variety of nutrients that might be burned or boiled out of the soil during the process) could be negligible. I decided (after comparing the garlics from the solarized box to the garlics from a box that had not been solarized) that to the eye there was no difference in size or appearance. But in taste? I'd have to be patient for another two weeks, when they'd be cured and able to be compared.

Will I solarize again next year?

I recalled the hours soaking the soil, the rolling out of the costly white plastic, the time and effort to hammer staples as the wind sought to snatch away my fingers as well as the plastic.

The task, carried through the described steps, required more than two hours of labor for a box.

I now had thirty boxes. Solarize all of them? Any of them?

No. Not again.

Experiment tried, experiment rejected.

If my work with garlic is only complicated by trying or continuing an experiment, the experiment has to be killed. The final test: might it bring me more bucks, so I could at least earn close to what I was spending?

Solarizing would fail the test.

Money spent that year: $2,356. Money earned: $1,779.

I knew my father was looking over my shoulder, checking my figures.

"So?" I heard him ask.

Don't ask. Not yet anyway.

On June 20 I began harvesting other boxes. By July 3, I'd pulled enough varieties of garlics from enough countries (nine) to satisfy the needs for the tasting at Oliveto.

In addition, I had the same amount of the same varieties in the process of curing so they'd be ready for delivery to Alice Waters at Chez Panisse in time for the Bastille Day dinner.

I have to admit I was impressed when I saw the festival's menus.

Until five or six years ago I had no idea what a tapenade was. A brandade was used to cover a scratch or cut on the finger. Confit? Concassee?

Oliveto, here I come.

FOR IMMEDIATE RELEASE
Contact: Eleanor Bertino, Denise Cody

Oliveto Garlic Week, July 25-31
Rare Garlics, Live Music, Children's Festivities

Garlic lovers of all ages, rejoice! Thirty varieties of garlic from around the world in special dishes and special menus, activities and entertainment for children, live music, and much more to take place at Oliveto Restaurant's Garlic Week, July 25-31.

The garlic used during the festival is organically grown by Chester Aaron in Occidental, California, and includes varieties from China, Korea, Persia, Israel, France, Italy, Russia, Poland and Mexico. Some, like Persian Star (Uzbekistan), Asian Tempest (South Korea), Metechi and Celaya Purple (Mexico), are rare if not exclusive to the western states. Currently, Aaron sells his limited delicacy only to Oliveto and Chez Panisse restaurants.

Sunday, July 25, 2:00 P.M.: Festivities kick off with entertainment for children by mime clown Christie Lewis, garlic art projects and peeling contests, followed by a family-style garlic harvest supper with live music by Parisian accordionist Odile Lavault. All children's activities are free. Dinner is $19 for adults and $12 for children. Seatings are at 5:00 and 7:00 P.M. and reservations are required. MENU ATT.

Saturday, July 31, The Garlic Gala: seatings at: 5:30-7:00 and 8:15-9:15 PM, a sumptuous five-course dinner with live "European cafe music" by La Cigalou. Second seating we'll roll out the dance floor. Price is $35 for the first seating and $45 for the second.

Monday-Friday, July 26-30: Special garlic dishes by Oliveto's reigning chef. John Harris, author of The Book of Garlic and publisher of *The Garlic Times,* will be guest host for the week—dispensing garlic lore and tastes, along with Oliveto owners Maggie and Bob Klein.

MENUS

Oliveto's Family-Style Garlic Harvest Supper
Sunday, July 25, 5:00 & 7:00 P.M.

Crostini with:
Brandade, white bean puree, roasted garlic, tomato confit,
eggplant caviar, tapenade, concassee of tomato, feta cheese, pesto

Choice of:
Spaghetti & meatballs, chicken with multiple cloves,
garlic pizza, with choice of:
Garlic-roasted zucchini, greens & garlic, broccoli with
garlic bread crumbs

Dessert:
Mixed-berry crisp with amaretti topping and
vanilla bean ice cream

Oliveto's Garlic Gala Dinner
Saturday, July 31, 5:30 and 8:15 P.M.

The Roasted, the Pickled, the Raw: A Garlic Sampler

A complimentary glass of fino sherry

Antipasti:
Garlic sausage with new red potato salad, tomato salad with garlic vinaigrette,
capers & chives, green bean salad with brown garlic chips and roasted red
peppers, garlic confit & pancetta tartlettes

Primi Piatti:
Fritto misto with calamari, shrimp & garlic fritters

Secondi piatti:
Grilled leg of lamb with Provencal mustard & garlic mashed potatoes
or
Poached sea bass in tomato and garlic with aioli & summer vegetables

Dessert:
Zabaglione or three sorbets (blackberry, plum, melon)
Fruit baskets and plates of truffles and cookies

CHAPTER 13

The Tasting

THE OWNERS AND CHEF AT OLIVETO were the first in the Bay Area to consider and then honor the fact that, like apples and pears and vegetables and fish and meat and, of course, wines, garlics come in many flavors.

I have never been a chef and, thank God, I never will be, but I have learned from experiences in Italy that food can be not just eaten but enjoyed, even celebrated.

All chefs will agree that garlic, ill used, can so dominate a dish that the specific flavor of the recipient pork or hen or sea bass or pasta never gets through to the palate. In such foods garlic is a tyrant.

After consuming food containing California White garlic, a certain taste and aroma remains on the gums, on the toothbrush, on the pillow, on the mustache, in the lipstick, in the armpit. Many garlic lovers consider this delayed effect an unavoidable or even an essential part of the experience.

Not so!

Maggie Klein, after travels in Morocco, Italy, Spain, and Portugal, wrote *The Feast of the Olive.* About ten years ago, Maggie and her husband Robert converted a piece of an old warehouse on College Avenue on the northern rim of Oakland into the closest thing to a Tuscan trattoria and ristorante to be found this side of Tuscany. There are small tables tucked under shaded arches or scattered in the sun on the wide sidewalks, ochre tiles on walls and floors, a polished bar, new paint that has attained a patina of age, and high, narrow windows like castle crenelations for pouring cappuccinos and lattes onto the masses below.

The obvious name for the cafe/restaurant: Oliveto.

I met Maggie and Robert (he has now progressed from partial to total involvement with operations) and visited Oliveto through the connivance of my former Saint Mary's College colleague, John Meis. In Italy, thanks to John, I ate food that sang grand opera. There I was, at the age of sixty, discovering that pasta should be tasted, not just scarfed up and swallowed, that fresh fruit and fresh vegetables and fresh herbs deserve the adoration due a remarkable woman or an exquisite ballet.

On the second day of my first visit to Italy, John drove me to Florence. At a curbside cart, he ordered, to my dismay and incipient nausea, a *panino* stuffed with *trippa*. Giovanni, the owner and our not-too-humble servant, is one of Florence's approximately forty such owners of mobile wagons called trippai ambulanti. These now modernized wagons, or vans, are manned (literally) by a descendant of the vendor who first claimed that same location five and six and seven generations before, when the wagon had a horse attached.

For this panino, Giovanni sliced a crunchy roll in half, pulled out the soft dough, stuck a fork in the top half of the roll, dipped it into a pot of warm broth to moisten the rim, and filled the cavity with a mix (sliced trippa, olive oil, vinegar, finely chopped onion, celery, carrot, garlic and parsley) that had been marinating for hours.

Trippa is tripe.

Tripe?

Tripe!

Tripe is the lining of the stomach of animals that chew their cud: sheep, goats, mainly cattle. For many tripe connoisseurs, the quality of the tripe depends on which animal is used, as well as which of the different compartments of the stomach.

Try it for yourself:

Tripe

(Serves 4-6)

2 pounds honeycomb tripe
4 whole cloves
½ teaspoon sugar
1 teaspoon salt
2 cups highly seasoned tomato sauce
1 green bell pepper, seeded, deveined, and diced
2 onions, diced
½ cup chopped celery
6 cloves Metechi or Mexican garlic, minced
¼ teaspoon dried thyme
1 large bay leaf
¼ teaspoon ground black pepper
1 pinch of cayenne pepper
freshly grated Parmesan cheese to taste

1. Wash the tripe several times under cold running water. Cut it into thin strips. Place the strips in a large sauce pan. Cover with cold water. Bring to a boil. Add the cloves, sugar, and ½ teaspoon of the salt. Cover and simmer for 2 to 3 hours, or until the tripe is tender. Drain.

2. Add the tomato sauce, bell pepper, onions, celery, garlic, thyme, bay leaf, remaining ½ teaspoon of salt, black pepper, and cayenne. Cover, simmer for 20 minutes. Remove bay leaf.

3. Serve hot, topped with grated cheese.

Incidentally, the garlics mentioned—Metechi or Mexican—are quite fiery.

After consuming the first panino, I ordered two more.

In mid-afternoon, at two different trippai ambulanti near the Duomo and then near the train station, I had a fourth and a fifth. Preparing to order a sixth, I acceded to John's warnings. We would be dining at his favorite restaurant in all of Tuscany, perhaps all of Italy. I might not have a very buon appetito were I to overindulge this late in the afternoon.

Indeed, at eight o'clock, at the indefatigable John's favorite restaurant, Cibreo, treasures appeared before my eyes and slowly, casually, not with truffles and flourishes but with a heartbreaking melange of strings—violins, perhaps an occasional cello—appeared and disappeared.

Oliveto's downstairs cafe offers moderate servings of Californized European foods suitable for snack or lunch, such as grilled eggplant with sundried tomatoes, a wild mushroom and herbed ricotta tart, and mango upside-down cake.

For heavy-duty fare, ascend the narrow, winding castle stairway leading from the cafe up to the restaurant. Just about everyone here is a devotee of garlic.

Master chef (and now partner) Paul Bertoli was formerly (for ten years) chef at Chez Panisse. He now creates the daily menu and oversees special events for Oliveto. He is direct, unassuming, honest, and a scholar as well as a culinary master.

Unlike most restaurants in Berkeley and San Francisco, the rule in Oliveto's kitchen is: No haggling with suppliers over the prices of vegetables, fruits, meats. Demand the best.

When I deliver a crate of free samples of my Hosui pears or red blue plumcots or Arkansas Black apples, the workers in Oliveto's kitchen actually know the English words that communicate gratitude. Respect for the supplier helped persuade me to concentrate the current and future sales of my garlic on Oliveto.

There is, in the kitchens of many well-known restaurants, a culture of condescension that patrons rarely witness. That condescension usually descends down the ladder of authority from chef to dishwasher, and too often finds a final defenseless target in the supplier. What scorn won't most suppliers accept just to be able to announce they are servicing this or that current icon of *Gourmet* magazine.

Fifty years ago I refused to indulge overbearing sergeants and colonels in combat and, more recently, in exchanges almost as deadly as combat, sanctimonious professors and writers. I certainly won't indulge silly little Yuppie wretches.

I have rigid rules about the food I eat, especially at restaurants where I'm expected to pay my monthly allowance for the primo piatto and my annual for the secondo piatto.

I do have the chutzpah to return a dish that could have been prepared at Burger King. I've had some tasty and filling and inexpensive meals at Burger King, but I have wept too many times when I calculated how many barbecued burgers I could have enjoyed with the check presented at San Francisco's Master's or Circle 2 or The Mayan Cafe.

For me, and for many with whom I've spoken, it is the kitchen at Oliveto, without the honeyed glitz of socialite editors and critics, that determines its current position as flagship of the Bay Area's food fleet.

Paul Bertoli's position at the wheel of that flagship defines the spirit of the kitchen and dining room. Perhaps because of his Italian ancestry, perhaps because he is a man of simple and elegant taste, probably because he is highly intelligent, certainly because he loves garlic as much as I do, or for other reasons, he draws attention from across the country (see the *New York Times,* September 6, 1994).

I've yet to meet an Oliveto patron who sneers or complains.

Except, of course, the time that I met a New Yorker.

The day of the tasting arrived. About fifteen food writers from Bay Area newspapers and magazines joined an almost equal number of chefs from upscale restaurants in Berkeley and San Francisco at Oliveto. In the center of a long table was a bouquet of California wildflowers. Around the table were fourteen large platters, each with a different variety of garlic. In front of each of the platters was a white card with fine black calligraphy identifying the individual platter's garlic. Thirteen platters held my garlic; the remaining one held California White.

Each garlic was offered in three separate bowls. One contained baked cloves, one garlic-rubbed bruschetta, and one chopped, raw cloves ready to be speared by a toothpick tip.

In front of each platter, next to the identifying card, was the finest and most colorful representative head I could find of that variety.

I can hear the college students in civics class, their text *Polls and How to Corrupt Them:* "Not a blind test! Not scientific! Prejudices inevitable!"

But these tasters are people whose careers depend on their having well-educated and objective palates. I'd trust them before I'd trust those "scientific" polls. Remember the geologists and physicists and chemists and astronomers who, at the time of the moon landing, babbled, "Bring back three stones and we'll tell you how the universe was created!"

Twenty-eight years and two trillion bucks and a million stones later, we're still waiting.

A woman named Anna, who owns one of the more distinguished restaurants in San Francisco, grabbed my arm, kissed my cheek, congratulated me. I was pleased to see her. Once I'd had a crush on Anna. A disciple of Alice Waters, she was the person who introduced me to California nouvelle cuisine, which I'd defined then as undercooked peas.

Recently, Anna and her husband joined me and twelve other guests at my home in Occidental. Nicole and Bob Wald had brought me a bottle of wine which, Bob informed me, was possibly the best of its kind available in the country today.

I wanted everyone present to have a taste of the wine. But I owned only six wineglasses, two of which had just been broken, and four of which were already in use. I'd been serving, to no complaint, both wine and beer in clear plastic glasses.

Anna complained.

She chastised me loudly and publicly for serving such a wine in plastic. It was, she said, gauche. I decided that I deserved Anna's scorn. Not because I was a hick but because I had actually *elected* to run in her circles.

Anna had owned a restaurant in Berkeley and then graduated to a fine new place in San Francisco that became so famous she was considered by a few to be in the same one-woman league as Alice Waters. At the drop of a piece of arugula, she would toss off such words as *aperitif, confit, aioli, bagna cauda.*

Once, when I went to her restaurant with a woman friend, Anna brought a red wine to my table and three glasses. She sat with us for a few minutes. The wine: a Bordeaux, Haut-Brion, '75.

"Look at that dark color, Chester. Very *solide*. Tremendous fruit, lots of tannin." I'd already ordered two glasses of 1974 Spring Mountain, but when she sat she pushed those glasses aside. "Sorry, Chester. Not the best. Has an attractive bouquet and some elegance, but it's a bit too dry for me."

Me, too, Anna, more than a bit too dry. Elegance? Slightly less than some.

"Try this, guys. A 1971 Gimmeldingen Biengarten Riesling Beerenauslese. Superb concentrated bouquet, sheer nectar, a truly magnificent wine."

Yeah.

When we happened to be at the same gatherings in San Francisco (we had mutual friends), Anna casually compared the service at the best restaurants in New York, Florence, Berlin, London. One night, a month after my humiliation by Anna in my own home, I joined mutual friends at her San Francisco restaurant for dinner. I ordered stuffed calamari.

Anna was the chef that evening.

The calamari arrived, each of them plump and tasty with an exquisitely savory (why, I can't remember) sauce. But each of my plump little squid, I promptly discovered, still contained its cuttlebone. I had three options: cut each beast open and remove the bone; submissively eat the damn thing and (to the discomfort of my tablemates) pull the bone from my mouth; swallow each remnant of gristle and face a trip to surgery.

My gruff, greasy, fishermen friends who drink local wine from jelly glasses or from the bottle would never have been so ignorant or so gauche as to serve calamari with the cuttlebone embedded.

My tongue almost bled from my biting it, but the restraint and pain did help me lose some of my awe of gourmands and gourmets and wannabes.

John and Denisen Eleanor and the Kleins had worked hard and well to prepare the tasting. Their invitations had brought in fifty highly respected chefs, food writers, and newspaper and magazine editors.

Like the general public, few were acquainted with any garlic but the standard Early or Late California White. Except for an occasional so-called Italian Red.

The two photographers moved through the room snapping their cameras at the people, at the sunstruck paneled walls, at the brass sconces, and at the grand table set with garlic platters, crackers, breads, and sticks of jicima root.

Click click click!

Fourteen platters of garlic. Click click click!

Names of garlic, white cards, thin beautiful calligraphy! Click click click!

Faces, gowns, beards, jewelry, big names, small names, no names. Click click click!

The king, John Harris. Click click click!

Maggie, Robert. Click click click!

John guided people through what would be the travel route for the tasting.

"In front of each large platter you'll find a single head of the variety of garlic contained on the platter. A card on the table identifies the garlic and the country of its origin. Compare the head to other heads: size, shape, colors.

"Each of the three smaller plates within each platter offers a different preparation of that garlic. Baked, rubbed on bruschetta, raw. There is a variety of unsalted crackers. There are sticks of jicima root available for cleansing the mouth whenever you feel the need. On the sideboard at the end of the room are eight different wines with which you may complement your tasting as you wish.

"There are fourteen platters, fourteen varieties of garlic. Thirteen of the varieties come from Chester Aaron's farm. The fourteenth, the California White, is the garlic you'll find in your supermarkets. It's from Gilroy.

"Each of you has a form for the taste test. Please complete it before you leave. My suggestion, and it's only a suggestion: Go around the table *smelling* each garlic first. Write some notes about your reactions. Then go round again, first tasting a small sample of the baked garlic on each platter so that your palate will not be burned. More notes. Next go-round:

taste the bruschetta, and take notes, then try it raw. If possible, please try to distinguish the intensity of the bite, how soon it hits, where it strikes, and how long it lasts. And try to discern and describe the different final tastes. More notes.

"After you've experienced enough of each of the fourteen varieties, would you please identify, in the appropriate place on the form, your favorite and least-favorite garlic. In the blank space will you please tell us why it is or is not your favorite.

"On the last page of the form: Please rank the garlics, your favorite being number one. Any other comments are welcome."

I tried to convince myself that all this was a game, that it ought to be fun. And yet, when I observed a small gathering of people stalled at each station, sniffing, nibbling, chewing, gulping, concentrating, aspirating over another nibble, I was almost ashamed of myself.

Paul Bertoli, surveying the table as if it were an important ancient map, renewed my sense of proportion.

Paul gave several serious moments to each platter. Sitting on a chair, he worked as John had suggested: baked garlic first, then the bruschetta, then raw. He tasted, concentrated, made notes, moved on to the next platter. This was not a social event for him. During the almost two hours of the tasting I watched him tour the table twice, tasting each garlic again, checking his notes, amending them.

He was not pretending, not trying to impress.

I could not help listening to the others discussing the event. This could easily have been a fine-wine tasting at a select cellar in Napa:

"...the early aroma, the approaching scent...the bite, the sting, the taste...this one lies on the tongue then bounces to the palate, that one stays at the back of the throat...the taste is light, evocative of late summer or early autumn, sweet and mild...coarse, buttery, lumpy, fine grained...large clove, small clove, sharp-tipped clove, blunt-tipped clove, round like a marble...rose color, brown skin, striped skin, purple, dark red, pink skinned, white porcelain skin...this would be a perfect garlic for salsa, I'd want this garlic for pasta sauce, divine for bruschetta, perfect as a savory for crisp, raw vegetables, so delicate, so mellow...but careful, it could be overwhelmed by certain herbs...."

I thought about how Poppa, if he were here, would travel up and down the table like a wolverine, shoving competitors aside, scarfing up garlic by the handful (all of it raw), heedless of the fine distinctions.

Maggie Klein dropped into a chair. She looked sick.

"Are you okay, Maggie?"

"Jesus. All this fucking garlic. It's just too much."

Maggie has no need to impress me or anyone else.

I knew that Denisen Eleanor had collected the forms from several of the people in the room. For some sense of the success of the tasting, and to verify the span of tastes of the varieties (and the span of their potential usage), later that afternoon we made hasty calculations in Maggie's office.

Remember that several of these garlics were pulled early and had little time to cure. And, as well, only a few of my intensely-rich Georgian and Asiatics were represented.

	Overall Points
Creole Red	9.25
Spanish Roja	7.25
Russian Red Toch	6.5
Rosewood	6.25
Celaya Purple	5.66
Polish Carpathian White	5.75
French Messadrone	5.25
Inchelium Red	4.5
California White	2.5

SELECTED COMMENTS

Creole Red

Appearance: Beautiful purple, deep red, symmetrical

Aroma & Taste: (Raw) mild at first, lingering aftertaste, hot;(cooked) rich, flavorful, mild caramel, not hot, mild, heat in the finish

Characteristics: Very agreeable, excellent quality, juicy, caramelized

Spanish Roja

Appearance: Purple golden, red purple, soft mauve

Aroma & Taste: (Raw) taste of the stalk (a little muddy), piquant finish, mild scent and taste, medium hot; (cooked) artichoke-like, fairly creamy, caramel taste, hot & nutty

Characteristics: Good quality

Russian Red Toch

Appearance: White bulb mixed with purple, medium size, large cloves, red skin

Aroma & Taste: (Raw) little aroma, mild, light finish, taste of the ground and stalk, somewhat like garlic salt; (cooked) mild, potato-like, light finish, sweet, a little bitter

Characteristics: Nice appearance

Rosewood

Appearance: Large, white bulb, beautiful cloves, red skin, nice mottled purple

Aroma & Taste: (Raw) very intense, strong flavor, dirty; (cooked) very hot, starchy, caramelized flavor, sweet, too mild

Characteristics: Excellent quality

Celaya Purple

Appearance: Small head, large, narrow cloves, pale, white

Aroma & Taste: (Raw) mild with mild finish, (cooked) mild flavor and finish, sharp, not interesting, strong and lingering

Characteristics: Textured in cooked state

Polish Carpathian Red

Appearance: Small head, purple skin, small, tight bulb

Aroma & Taste: (Raw) like a hot chile, could be painful for some, strong garlic smell; (cooked) mild, not very rich, hot finish

Characteristics: Gritty and hot. Doesn't roast well

French Messadrone

Appearance: Large artichoke bulb

Aroma & Taste: (Raw) slightly hot, nice texture; (cooked) soft, retains traces of bitterness, creamy, light

Characteristics: Spiky cloves, very creamy and moist in cooked state, vibrant

Above: Sheltered by Asian pear trees, my cloves receive drip irrigation.

Left: First harvest, 1992.

Left: Two varieties of garlic, both from Washington State.

Below: My 1991 garlic was unsuccessfully protected by bird netting.

Planting cloves in holes punched through newspaper.

Inchelium Red

Appearance: White, tight head, medium cloves

Aroma & Taste: (Raw) hot up front, surprisingly mild in flavor, light watery flavor; (cooked) creamy, mild, not special, excellent flavor, hot finish, soft flavor

Characteristics: Nice appearance

California White

Appearance: Small, tight head, medium cloves

Aroma & Taste: (Raw) mild, medium strength flavor, slightly salty; (cooked) full, piquant finish (strong!), chemical, not appetizing, not rich, mild acidic taste

Characteristics: Flat

I left Oliveto soon after the tasting and took my time driving home. Sure, I was pleased. I could even admit that it had been fun. But something was bothering me and I couldn't figure out what it was.

At Mill Valley I took the route over the mountains to the ocean and drove the rest of the way north along the coast on Highway 1. It was mid afternoon and the beaches were filled. Traffic was heavy, so each curve of the narrow road had its ration of anxiety. North of Bolinas the traffic thinned out. By the time I arrived in Point Reyes, the friendly fog appeared and the breeze turned cool. I considered the afterglow of the tasting and tried again to understand my discontent. Hadn't everything worked out well? My garlics had more than proven themselves. Maybe I was just exhausted; maybe I had a touch of the flu.

The majority of the tasters had rated Creole Red and Spanish Roja number one and number two. I had predicted that. But I'd predicted number three would be the mild, almost apple-sweet Inchelium Red, from Washington. Their choice for third: Red Toch, from the Republic of Georgia.

I had hoped, of course, Red Toch would have been selected number one. To me, it was and is.

Tochliavari. I continued the drive north along the coast, remembering my father.

The weather turned cooler as I headed north through the hills of northern Sonoma County, where sheep and cattle searched the brown fields for remnants of the bales of clover dropped earlier that morning. By the time I reached Valley Ford and turned inland I had to turn on the heater.

Momma and Poppa would have wept at the beauty of this land, these obedient hills that waited like well-trained and contented animals.

Momma and Poppa.

There! *That* was what was bothering me.

As proud as they would have been at the respect offered me and my work at Oliveto a few hours ago, Momma and Poppa would have been concerned. Had the reception, the tasting, convinced me to *continue* growing garlic? Maybe even to expand?

My mother's voice found its way west. "Chester, my darling, you give so much time to garlic. So what happens, my darling? What happens is you spend not so much time you write books." Books.

Were my mother and father alive now to advise me they would finally agree on something. "Go on, go on. Write books. Garden? Plant? Garden? Plant? Now, then, a little, a bit maybe, sure. But books...ah."

They had always held any book, no matter its message or its value, as if it were a piece of the Torah.

Anyone, everyone, can dig in the earth. In a backyard, a field, a jar, a small square of yard in a tenement, or a prairie, whoever wants to can grow something.

But how many can mine words?

Heinrich Heine once wrote that the Jews, when they were driven from their land, left behind them all their riches and took into exile only one possession: the book.

Go, make your book, Chester.

Momma and Poppa rode with me in my car across the magnificent California land, through the cattle-filled meadows, past the herds of innocent sheep, into the dark redwoods.

I drove through the redwoods and into Occidental, up past Liza's vineyard (with two Arabian mares almost obscured as they grazed among the vines) and down the dirt road to my house—the fields spread out around my garlic, my fruit trees playing host to several big-eared deer, the sun down but still throwing red light over the ridges—going slowly, seeing, hearing, smelling.

I yielded to an ache so severe that I wept like a deserted baby.

I wept not from the pain but from the realization of all my unused, undeclared love for my parents. I will carry this unspent love into my grave. It will follow my soul whether it falls or rises.

Well, boychik, thank God it's not hate.

I walked down the path to the house. I fed Sadie, climbed the stairs, undressed. There were several messages on my machine.

The first one was the voice of Mary Catherine O'Connor.

"Dear man. I am so proud of you. You were so casual. I watched you admire the beautiful women. I wasn't concerned at all. I think I love you."

I had no need to play the other messages then.

Tomorrow.

Chapter 14

The Prayer of the Horseshoe

The next morning I was surprised to find new and unusual voices on my machine.

"Chester Aaron, I'm back home in Denver. Just spent a few days in San Francisco last week. Read the newspaper. The article about garlic. Are you the Chester Aaron from Butler, Pennsylvania? Are you Ray Aaron's brother? You have to be. Do you remember Mike Halahurich? You went with my cousin Juley Fako. Remember me? Played football with Ray in high school, then semi-pro. How is Ray? Will you call Mike Halahurich, please? Jesus, I couldn't believe it when I read that article in the *San Francisco Chronicle.* It took me back maybe sixty years. I remember you. You were twelve, maybe fourteen. A scrappy little bastard. Ray talked about you all the time. You were gonna be a writer, he said. So you're a farmer? I got the right guy? You can call collect. Okay? Okay, Chester?"

You bet I remember Mike Halahurich. You bet I remember Juley Fako. And Helen Sopel. And Juley Galida.

Mike forgot to leave his number in Denver. I called information. No Halahurich, Mike or Michael, was listed in Denver.

...gonna be a writer...so you're a farmer...

Do I want to track him down this morning? I'd have to try to explain, to legitimize, my betrayal to my brother Ray. And to me?

Mike, I can't explain my confusion to myself, how can I explain it to you?

Later. Tonight perhaps.

Next message: Alexei, whose father, he shouts at me, was also born in Soviet Georgia. Currently, he shouts at me, he lives about ten miles north of Occidental, in Santa Rosa. He'd read the article in the *Chronicle.*

"Help me," he shouts into the box of cables within my machine. "Every year I plant garlic just like my father planted. Every year okay. Suddenly this year nothing."

I call Alexei.

He compliments me on my fame and then informs me that his wife won the bet.

"The bet?"

"Yeah. I said you'd be too famous to talk *neizvestno s kem.*"

"Pardon me?"

"I won this one. I bet her you don't speak Russian. Neizvestno s kem. Shame on you. Means, you know, *just with anybody.* She said you sounded like a good person in that article in the *San Francisco Chronicle.* She kept telling me to be patient, you'd call. She won that one. She's an optimist, she ain't Russian."

After five minutes of his checking my Georgian credentials and making sure I am not really an Armenian, I manage to get the idea across that my time is limited. "Okay," he shouts at me, "I know you're busy. But I got problems. *Chesnok.* I've been planting it five years now."

"Chesnok. Garlic."

"Good. Very good."

I tell him I have a garlic called Chesnok Red. "It's from Georgia."

"I know about Russian Red. Five years I've picked up Russian Red at different farmer's markets. So I know about Russian Red."

"There are twenty or thirty *so-called* Russian Reds. Where in the USSR did your Russian Red garlic come from?"

"Whatta you mean? It comes from USSR. Like I said."

"That's what the guy who sold it to you told you. Well, the USSR is a huge country, a hundred cultures. I've got twelve different garlics from there, six from Soviet Georgia alone. They all look different, they all taste different."

"You telling me about Georgia? I know Georgia. And what the hell kind of Georgian are you? Georgia's not Soviet anymore. We're independent. We're a separate republic. We're free."

"We? What I'm saying is..."

"I know what you're saying. I tell you it's Russian Red. The guy at the farmer's market says that's what it is. He's from the Ukraine."

"Okay. What's the problem, Alexei?"

"The heads I grow are always smaller than ones I get from that guy at the market and plant. *Chto zhe u menya tut ne tak*?"

"English?"

"What am I doing wrong?"

"Maybe it's not you, maybe it's the garlic. Are you planting in containers or in the ground?"

"Oh, I know about *susliki*. Gophers. If that's what you're thinking. Hey, I only live ten miles from you. You got gophers, I got gophers. That article in the *Chronicle*. I know. I plant containers, like you do. Wire bottoms."

"Do you fertilize?"

"Sure I fertilize. I know about fertilizer. I got twenty chickens. Chicken fertilizer's the best."

"Actually rabbit or goat is better. You don't use the manure hot, do you? I mean fresh."

"Of course I don't. I know what hot means, I know about fresh manure. Fresh manure burns vegetables. Stuff I use is aged maybe six months."

"The rule of hand is you should add about thirty pounds to a thirty-cubic-foot space."

"What do you think my chickens are? Ostriches? I got twenty bantams. In two years I don't get ten pounds from the whole flock. I practically scrape it up with a razor blade."

"How many containers? How big are they?"

"Oh, I know about containers. That what you're getting at? They're too wide you can't reach the center rows from either side. Right? That what you're getting at?"

"How wide? How long?"

"Four feet wide, eight feet long, six inches high. I use 2 X 6. Redwood scrap lumber. Redwood's more expensive now than my daughter. She's away at college. What good college'll do her you can blow into your handkerchief. She'll get that degree and work at some cafe, a waitress."

Where had I heard that contemptuous putdown before?

"Okay, Alexei. One thing: your boxes are not high enough. Use 2 X 12. Gophers can get over a six-inch height. Next thing, I'd guess you're not using enough manure. Do you water?"

"Every day. I know about watering. I have a drip system. Designed it myself. I know more about drip than those *duraki* at the hardware stores. You know what it means duraki? Fools."

"What size are your emitters? How far apart? How long does the system drip? How many lines to your four-foot-wide box?"

"I use my drip every morning. Run it for two hours."

"Every day is probably too much. I don't know your soil and I don't know your drip system, but I'd guess..."

"Hell, my soil's like your's. Clay."

"Which means the water's not penetrating. It's running off. I've built up my soil over four years with manure and compost and cover crops. Now there's very little clay. On clay soils, I'd suggest you think about in-line tubing with 1/2-gph emitters on twelve-inch intervals. In a 4 x 8-foot box I'd suggest three lines of tubing..."

"I have five lines. Don't want to take any chances. And I water every day. Anyway, I don't know anything about that gph bullshit. I'm ordinary joe. Gph. What the hell's gph?"

"Gph means gallons per an hour. I'd suggest building up your soil. Soil needs tilth. I'd also suggest watering every three or four days for no more than an hour each day. Push your finger down in the soil. Soil should be consistently moist, not soaked. Shouldn't go dry between waterings. Do you stop watering before you pull the garlic?"

"Sure I do. I know about drying out the garlic. I let it sit in the ground for maybe a month, six weeks, drying out. What's that word you said? Filth?"

"Tilth. The condition of the soil. Soil with good tilth is loose, easily penetrated by roots, easy to break, easy to crumble or crush in your hand. Clay has no tilth. Did you say the garlic sits in the ground six weeks drying out?"

"Four, maybe six weeks. Yeah."

"Too long. Two or three weeks in the soil at the most, after the leaves start browning. Longer than that the bulbs begin to bake in the ground. Harvest when about three fourths of the leaves have gone brown. When do you plant?"

"I know about planting. The old country way. Full moon, June or July."

"Too early. Around here October, November is the ideal time. The clove needs coldest possible weather to build up strength and put down roots. If you plant your garlic in June or July, when do you pull it?"

"Six, seven months later. December, January."

"Too soon. You said you withdraw water."

"I do. I stop my drip early December."

"But there are rains in December and January. Often in November."

"Hell yes, there are rains. A man can't control the weather. I wasn't a Catholic...Russian Orthodox, I tell you...I'd say I don't think even God controls the weather."

"Look, give me your address and I'll mail you information, some notes about what I think you should be doing. Meantime, go to a bookstore and buy a book called *Drip Irrigation* by Robert Kourik and..."

"I don't go to bookstores. Been reading *Reader's Digest* for forty years. Not gonna stop now and go to a bookstore."

"What's your address?"

"Okay. You won't just screw off and never put this in the mail, will you?"

"I called back, didn't I? Tell me, why do I have the feeling I ought to be thanking you for calling me?"

"You want to send me that book by Koolik?"

"No. You'll have to buy it yourself. And the name's Kourik. Robert."

He speaks Russian for a minute or two, none of which I understand, then he deigns to give me his address.

His Russian sounds legitimate. I think he is calling me a phony Georgian. Or maybe a typical Russian. He doubts my spirit of charity. I actually almost apologize, almost admit my own failure to appreciate his problems, almost request his permission to come visit him, to plant his garlic for him, to *give* him garlic. I catch myself in time.

"One last thing, Alexei. You said you plant in boxes."

"Yes, of course in boxes. What other choice do I got? In the air?"

"Have you seen signs of gophers in your boxes?"

"Some. Actually many more this year than last year or the year before."

"Alexei, kill the little buggers."

"I don't kill anything, not even flies. I'm Georgian. Georgians don't kill gophers or flies."

Unable and unwilling to go political or to pop him with psychology, I give him a few pointers and try to excuse myself. I don't dare ask him if he's been reading about what the Georgians are doing to each other and to others. But in what I take to be a perverse need for punishment, I almost prolong the conversation in the hopes that he'll speak more Russian. I am surprised at how much of what he says I understand or get the sense of. I haven't heard the language very often the past few years. When I did, I paid little attention to it. Now the sound of his words, the unyielding righteousness of his manner, make me homesick. Not so much homesick as father sick.

The man's gruff, ornery arrogance gives birth to an image of my father. Try to tell my father anything about anything he didn't know anything about, you'd get your head snapped off.

Poppa, the store's losing money...*I know the store's losing money* ...Poppa, if you stopped trusting customers who haven't paid you for five years you'd...*They get work they'll get money, they get money they'll pay. I know workers. All over the world workers are the same*...But for as long as I remember you've been saying the workers everywhere are out to rob and kill the Jews...*So? Prove I'm wrong. Prove it, smart high school graduate, prove it*...But I don't have to be a businessman to know...*You're grown up, boychik, you're a businessman, you're successful, you make a profit every year, you come give me advice I'll listen...*

Next message: "Hey, man, I'm from Ventura, around Los Angeles. Name's Alvin. I have a couple acres out in the boonies. This is my second year growing garlic. I sell it to the Korean shopkeepers. I'm a black man but I'm an equal opportunity seller, man, but the Koreans don't want to pay what I'm asking. That's okay. We've had troubles down here, you know, and I'm sort of a missionary between the races. I need advice. Saw your story in the *Chronicle*. About growing this beautiful stuff called garlic. Story blew my mind, man. I'm on my way to Point Arena. Got a buddy there. A fisherman. Drove over to Occidental to call you. You're not home. Damn. Call me, okay? Hey, man, call collect."

I call Alvin in Point Arena, where he said he'd be staying with his fisherman friend.

Alvin answers. "Hey, man, I was just about to call you. We're on our way out to sea in an hour. Fishing. You home day after tomorrow? I'm driving south. I mean to stop in Occidental and visit you, man. I've got dreams, I've got ambitions. Please be there. You're gonna change my life, man."

Alvin does visit me two days later. He calls me from the village. I drive down. Tall, muscled, with dreadlocks that would divert a hurricane. I drive him back to my house.

We walk through the meadow, stopping at every box of garlic. He reads every plastic label placed in every box, occasionally two or three labels to a box. He asks at least fifty questions, all of them important, in a voice so jubilant he sounds like a teenager. Which he surely isn't.

Released from prison a year ago, he informs me, he is now living free, married, on about ten acres near Ventura. He wants to go straight, wants to work outside, wants to become a farmer, to make himself some honest money. He loves garlic, eats garlic like it's candy. He intends to grow garlic and sell it.

We drink coffee on the deck, I give him some articles from catalogues, pack about ten pounds of garlic (six different varieties) into a box, and drive him back to the village.

On the way down the hill my curiosity gets the better of me. "How'd you get interested in garlic, Alvin?"

"Food, man. In prison everyone divides his time between thinking about pussy and thinking about food. Next to *Penthouse* and *Playboy* the most popular magazine is *Gourmet* magazine. I subscribed to the *Los Angeles Times* just for their food section. Had photographs of food on my walls next to the beaver shots. When I read about you the other day I thought: There's my savior. And you know, you're everything I'd hoped you'd be. Swear to God. Hey, tell me about elephant garlic."

"Most purists look down their noses at it. It's mild, not really garlic. It's a leek."

"People buy it like mad in L.A. No wonder. They're leaks, too. Not authentic. But the stuff sells, man. I am gonna grow me some."

"Do it. Don't listen to purists. Purists are like fundamentalist Jews, Christians, Muslims, carpenters. They know everything. They're clean. Everyone else is evil."

"Growing garlic does this to a man?"

"Does what?"

"Makes a man a philosopher. I'm goin' for it, man. I've always wanted to be a gourmet philosopher. I want to do you back."

"Nah. No need."

"Tell you what. I got a ten-year collection of *Penthouse*. I'll send you half. Five years."

"Alvin, I'm in love. I have a marvelous woman."

"Okay, I'll think of something."

Next message: efficient, managerial, a bit over-cheery. It's the owner of a new hotshot deli just opening in Beverly Hills. Will I call her back? "The famous people…film people, you know…they'll find your exotic garlic very chic. Hope you don't charge too much."

No.

Next: "Hey, Chester. This is Louis. Give me a call. The kids and Susan want to come up and work. All goes well here. We miss you, and we sure as hell do continue to love you. Don't ask me why."

Louis, my son. My darling, as Momma would say.

On the deck I take out a small brown envelope given to me by a woman last night at the tasting. A woman named Susan Black. She'd just returned from Mexico, heard about the tasting and searched me out. She talked of a tiny garlic she'd discovered in Mexico, calling it magic Mexican garlic.

Susan Black wrote, in an enclosed note, that she'd found this garlic in a large common market, where it was available not among the ordinary foods but in the herb and charm stalls. She was giving me the only four cloves she had.

Those cloves were about the size of the marbles I used to play with as a child. On examination I thought they might be too far gone to plant, but perhaps I'd give them a try. Why not?

"I've also enclosed one of the religious articles that uses the same single round bulb. This one is many years old. I call them garlic Jesuses but I only know the garlic is used to ward off evil and bring good luck. Seems quite reliable."

Fixed to a flat piece of cardboard about the size of a playing card and encased in plastic is a very small horseshoe wrapped with copper wire. Beneath the horseshoe: an armor-crested, red-robed knight/saint, brandishing a sword as he reins in a glossy-brown mare. Also inside the plastic, in their own little envelope, are what look like caraway seeds. (To ward off bad breath?)

A garland of fifteen tiny garlic cloves, wound through with bright red ribbon, is fixed to the card, on top of the plastic wrap. A handmade hook has been fashioned from wire so the charm might be hung from a doorknob.

Six months after the tasting, after Susan Black's offering, a friend named Annie, who worked at the Union Hotel Cafe, translated the Spanish message printed on the back of the charm.

Here is an excerpt from that message, which is titled "The Prayer of the Horseshoe:"

For the Holy Trinity, Horseshoe, I christen you
in the name of the Father, the Son, and the Holy Spirit;
give me good luck, health, and money: when you went
through the wilderness, Saint Santiago, through thorns
and weeds, you blindfolded your enemies' eyes with
your great power. I want you to, just like you put this
horseshoe on your horse and with it liberated yourself
from that wilderness, just like that, I want this horseshoe
to give me luck, health and money, through the power
that God has given you...May this horseshoe give me
everything I want, may it help me disappear out of danger
without anyone noticing, may it help me come up with
money and honors, may it help me be loved by all
those whom I love, or want to be loved by, liberate me
from all of my enemies and fatal dangers...

AMEN.

I planted the four cloves. They never came up. When I harvested in 1994 I could not find them in the soil. Bad luck?

Now, almost three years later, Janice Dent, who owns a cafe called Local Color in Occidental and sells an earth-shaking sandwich of roasted turkey and roasted garlic, returned from a village in Mexico. She'd smuggled across the border, just for me, a gift of ten garlic cloves she'd found in a market stall.

It is the same garlic. In October all ten cloves went into box No. 38.

Good luck? I'll know in about ten months.

Please, Saint Santiago, I want money and honors too. I also want to be loved by all whom I love. I even want to be loved by those I hate.

Thank you, Saint Santiago.

Poppa, I hear your damn Pi-tooey!

CHAPTER 15

Fame... and Fortune?

I AGREED TO PAUL BERTOLI'S REQUEST to supply him with green garlic this year for his Italian spring-green garlic soup. The demand for that soup last year had overwhelmed Oliveto's kitchen. I must admit I also agreed to supply the greens because last year I alone, over three consecutive dinners, must have consumed a gallon of the stuff.

"Green garlic" refers to the green leaves sprouting up out of the clove, which are cut before the clove expands into a full head (of four or six or eight or more cloves); it is usually cut around early to mid-April.

What would the garlic of choice be?

If I'd had enough Russian Red Toch I'd have submitted it for the tasty sacrifice, but I'd only saved ten heads from last year. Ten heads, at eight or nine cloves a head, would not produce a fraction of the amount Paul needed. Nor could I just casually eliminate the garlic without metaphorically saying farewell again to my father.

I relied on Paul, who had his own favorite: Spanish Roja.

Spanish Roja it would be.

I felt neither maternal nor paternal affiliation to Spanish Roja. I liked it as a garlic, but it was not Georgian, after all. Also, I had several hundred heads available, more than enough for both regular and green specimens.

One of my boxes normally takes between 100 to 130 cloves, depending on the variety and the eventual size of the matured head. For a massive head, such as Leningrad or Dukanskij or Medidzhvari or Inchelium Red, the ratio is smaller: eighty to a hundred heads to a box. For Spanish Roja it's about 110 cloves.

To grow the garlic for the greens only (because no space is required for the expanding heads) the box can be jammed with four to five hundred cloves, one or two inches apart instead of the usual eight.

For someone like me, a small farmer, the elements of profit and loss have to be considered. The percentage of acceptable loss is lower for me than it is for a farmer with thousands of acres and a wife and six sons and daughters to absorb the labor.

Each 4 x 10-foot box will produce approximately forty pounds of greens. That same box would produce about seventy to eighty pounds of mature garlic heads. Charging the usual price for a pound, green or matured, means I'd be losing at least a hundred dollars on each box of greens. And I'd be losing potential seed.

My father, aware of my plans, of course, is shouting a planetary *pitooey!* at my gullibility and sentimentality. *What do restaurants care you dig in the hot sun all day? You think they think you work? No. You get it like they get it. Without bending your back or walking in mud. They care? Bah! Listen, boychik, do what your momma your poppa tell you. Go write that book.*

In late February I began to fear not just for the boxes of green garlic but for my entire crop.

From late January through late February there were twenty-six straight days of rain. Floods were severe throughout Sonoma County. Because of the sloping meadow, however, the water did not sit on my land. And because my crop was contained in boxes twelve inches above the soil, not a clove of garlic was washed away. I had less reason than others to worry.

The Russian River, fifteen miles from Occidental, crested and spread out over the lowlands, filling hundreds of homes with mud or washing them away. National news showed families in Guerneville struggling to survive. Hundreds of homeless, who'd lost all but the clothes on their bodies, were taken in by people and organizations in Occidental as well as Sebastopol and Santa Rosa.

One week later, I rise from my bed at six o'clock, just as the alarm goes off.

It is still dark, still cold, and the wind whips the rain so hard against the south wall I fear for my solar windows. The weather report indicates that the storm will continue through the rest of the week, with fifty- or even sixty-mile-an-hour winds. That's almost cyclone force.

The homes along the Russian River in Guerneville, those that had survived the flood of a week before, are in danger again. Refugees from the Russian River who'd returned home are again being cared for in Sebastopol and Occidental. The roads are so deep in water and mud I can drive no more than a few yards from my house.

When I walk among my boxes to gauge possible crop damage, I sink into muck a foot above my ankles. With each step I have to brace myself, to clutch the rims of my boots so the muck won't suck off the boot when I lift my foot.

My garlic cloves must be sinking fast. Have they already begun to rot?

Sadie cowers in her tent. She leaves its protection once or twice a day for a brief view, through the living room windows, of the rain striking deck and glass and the redwood branches whipping the deck. Secure in my living room, warmed by the fire in the iron stove, she has no desire to go off into any other room or closet in the house.

She ignores the litter box until she can stand it no longer. Sometimes at night I hear her meowing, probably in pain, and I have to visit her and pet her for a few minutes and carry her bodily from her tent to the litter box, where, if I remain close by, she'll relieve herself. After a hasty sanitary wash, she rushes again to her tent.

I am using my last set of sheets and longjohns. All roads to Sebastopol are flooded, so I cannot drive to town to attempt a long-overdue laundry. I, and hundreds of others, rely on Gonella's General Store in Occidental for candles and lamp fuel and batteries, just in case. And canned food. Electric lines in most of the flatland are down; propane tanks are empty. The three restaurants in town stay open long hours for those who, for whatever reasons, cannot cook at home. Late at night, several patrons at the Union Hotel Pizzeria, including me, admit that we're here because we're too depressed to deal with the task of preparing meals at home. Like several others unable to drive the flooded roads, I walked the two miles through the rain. Each of us needs to hear voices, needs to know that we are not coping with the wind and rain by ourselves.

Finally, after the fourth or fifth cup of coffee—warm, not hot, but better than cold—I secure my rain gear and walk the two miles home. Shelly, at the Pizzeria, has given me two batteries for my flashlight out of the supply of batteries they've been hoarding.

—

At five Saturday morning, the sound of my alarm wakens me. I lie in the darkness, listening to the rain. I turn on the switch of the bedside lamp, but there is no light.

I look out of my bedroom windows, at Robin's house on the other side of the meadow. There are always lights in her house at this hour, but now it is dark. I lift the phone to call my utility company. The phone is dead.

Dressed, I manage, with the help of my flashlight, to feed Sadie. She's not interested. She too, is bored with this aquatic life. She sniffs the kibble and walks with stiff legs back to her tent, ignoring me, as if despairing of my ever again fulfilling my purpose: guaranteeing her contentment.

In my boots and rain gear, relying on my flashlight, I walk down the road, hoping to find a neighbor who might have information about the power. Headlights down the road grow brighter as I approach. Two pickups are parked at the head of my lane, their lights pointing at four huge fir trees that have fallen, knocking out power and phone lines.

Several neighbors are working in the rain, moving, in their hooded gear and boots, like drunken moon walkers. Three chain saws are grinding their way through the tree trunks. Those of us not working the saws pull severed limbs away, drag them to the side, stack them as neatly as we can. When it grows light enough to see what we're doing, the owners of the pickups turn off their lights.

After two more hours the road is cleared enough so anyone who chooses to do so can drive down the hill to the Union Cafe, which operates on its own generator. I join four other men and two women in a jeep, and we share a prayer that the cafe's generator is still functioning. It is.

The lights in the cafe are dim but they are lights. There is enough power to heat the water for consecutive pots of coffee. No one talks about anything except their own private bottomless bag of miseries. Several women have brought their children, who are pasty gray and hollow eyed, as if they've not slept for days.

From the cafe's telephone I call Robert, who lives about five miles up in the hills. He has both power and a live phone. I should bring my laptop computer and whatever food I have and stay as long as necessary. His four-wheel drive Nissan can get me to my house. He arrives at the cafe in about half an hour.

Necessary ends up meaning two nights. During the days, Robert takes me to my house to feed the forlorn Sadie and clean her litter box. She does not even peek out of her tent to question me. When I stroke her head and coo sweet nothings, she does not purr.

The third night, as the storm lightens, I stay home. For Sadie. I walk down the hill to the cafe. On the way back I walk through rain so cold and wind-driven that I have to close my eyes to a squint so I can see any live wires that might be lying in the water. In the stretch of road where the four trees had fallen, another larger tree is down, lying like a mortally wounded dinosaur across the road. Climbing through the branches to get to the clear side is not unlike my basic training in the infantry. I was nineteen then, and the task was a bit easier.

I feed Sadie, hold her for several minutes, talk to her, and leave her to her own devices (several cloth mice rubbed with catnip). I build a fire for her. Why not?

This time, four of us work to clear the road, including the man who owns the land from which all the trees have launched their attacks.

His own house is about thirty yards in from the road. As we work we hear a crack, like a rifle shot, then several louder cracks accompanied by a low growl. The growl rises to a whine. The four of us stand, mute, paralyzed, watching a giant fir fall in slow motion toward his house.

The man screams and runs. We all chase after him.

The tree has sliced down through the roof and continued on through the second floor, to stop about four feet above the table where his wife and very young children had been sitting. A paperback copy of *Charlotte's Web* lies on the table, open to page 31. A branch has impaled the book, fixed it to the table.

I return to Robert's house, collect my possessions, and return home. Perhaps I can soothe my cat, who, I know, is even more terrified than I am. Perhaps, as she has so often done, she can soothe me.

For the next three days I live without power or phone, collecting buckets of rainwater so I can flush the toilets, writing at the dining table with help from six candles, each backed by a sconce made of aluminum foil, which doubles the intensity of the light, and eating cereal with bananas and milk. Everything in the refrigerator has spoiled and has been packed in plastic bags for an eventual trip to the dump. My last bottle of milk, held in the refrigerator until the last moment, is lukewarm.

In bed during the afternoon of the fourth day I am awakened by the sound of a radio. Power has been restored. While I am lying there, wondering if I even want to get out of bed, the phone rings. The Schwerins, in New York, are on the line. Judy Feiffer calls. My relatives in Los Angeles call. My son calls from Oakland. Even my ex-wife calls. They have been watching the news reports on television and have been trying to reach me for days.

We are all relieved that I'm alive.

Throughout the following weeks of spring I hear of neighbors whose grapes and vegetables have been ruined. The wind and rains have knocked all the blossoms off the fruit trees. No bees had appeared to pollinate, even had there been blossoms available. The ground is still soaked two, three, and four feet down. Several farmers, having lost their crops, will go into debt, and might have to sell out.

Small farmers like myself might lose a crop and a couple hundred bucks, but bigger growers are in trouble. A couple I know, two young, idealistic optimists, had bought land three years ago a mile north of me. They'd borrowed money to build a house. They'd cut and crosscut and fertilized the soil until last spring, when they bought five hundred bare-root peach trees. Those who knew better could have told them, but who could have predicted this turn of weather? Peach trees do not appreciate having their feet wet, let alone soaked. In April, when they should have been blooming, the trees were dead.

The young couple sold their land and home and, deep in debt, returned to Denver.

The second week of April, I go to the two boxes containing Paul Bertoli's garlic greens. What, I wonder, will I find?

The stalks are tall and vibrant green. When I pull them up and out of the mud the cloves are dark red, swollen, ready to burst. The root hairs are six to ten inches long. I taste a green blade; the garlic taste is strong but very soft.

I pull the garlic from the two boxes, greens and bulbs. Their total weight: eighty-two pounds.

The green garlic soup served at Oliveto in late April deserved a gold medal.

In late June, the sun is high and hot.

I remove my shirt and go to work, inserting the tines of the spade at the correct angle, so they reach under the garlic heads in box No. 1 but do not go deep enough to tear the gopher wire.

This garlic is Spanish Roja.

I tilt the spade and lift heads free. I advance along the length of the box until all the stalks are lying on the surface. Then I start tying them, five stalks to a bunch.

Twenty bundles.

Before I go on to box No. 2 (also Spanish Roja) I cover the bundles just pulled with burlap, to protect them from the sun.

When I pull and tie all the stalks in box No. 2, I haul them by wheelbarrow (a total of forty-two bundles) to my curing shed. Each bundle receives a tag containing the pertinent details: the name of the variety (Spanish Roja), the numbered box in which it grew (Box 1 or Box 2), the date it was planted (October 15, 1995), and the date it was harvested (June 21, 1996).

In three weeks, after the garlic has hung, greens and all, from wires, I will compare the heads of one variety (Creole Red, for example) grown in box No. 3 or 6 or 7, with other heads of Creole Red grown in other boxes with different soil mixes. This will help me make decisions about preparing the soils for the planting in October.

After two weeks of curing, each bundle will be removed from the wire and freed of greens and roots, and each head will be carefully cleaned and stored in the loft of my shed until I make my first delivery to Oliveto.

I work through lunch, into the mid afternoon, when, hot and burned and soaked, my body begins to run down. I have to take a break. Sadie, who'd been overseeing my progress the entire morning, runs ahead of me, knowing that the house will be at least thirty degrees cooler than the fields. She probably refuses to credit my solar heating, which is designed to cool the house in summer and heat it in winter. I'm sure she takes the credit: it's her home after all.

Eventually, after having built two more redwood boxes, after having added a ton of chicken manure to the soil in all forty boxes, having turned the soil in each box, having set up my drip irrigation again, and having filled each of my forty boxes with French shallots and cloves of garlic, I struggle each morning with my conscience.

What about my writing?

Another winter.

Outside the mist turns into drizzle, and the drizzle becomes serious rain. My left boot leaks: my foot's getting wet. Glum, a bit angry, my raincoat glossy slick, I collect and stack bits and pieces of lumber scattered across the lower field, haul fragments of black plastic (blown by the winds to every corner of my land) to the side of my garlic shed, and stuff them into garbage cans. Remnants of chicken wire left over from the work on the two newest and final boxes are folded and stacked and set near the garbage cans. As soon as the storm ends, I'll make a run to the county dump.

Above the road, I examine the six peach trees. After their leaves fell in October, I'd sprayed them to fight off the peach-leaf curl that, along with the severe storms, had reduced July's crop to less than a pound of wrinkled runts that tasted like olives.

This year, as soon as the leaves dropped, I'd mixed and sprayed the peach and nectarine trees with a solution of copper and sulfur, a nontoxic mix permitted by both the Agricultural Department and the Certified Organic Association. The blue tint of the copper is still visible on the bark. Are the viruses sleeping in the soil, recovering strength for an assault on my trees again in five months?

My mother was orderly, disciplined. Everything in her kitchen and her life had its place. When she crocheted she opened the certain drawer in the certain cabinet where all the required materials were contained. Needles, threads, patterns, squares of that particular netted cloth required for such work, fragments of designs begun and not yet completed. Everything was in the same place every time.

And yet she never complained about my father's inability to keep even a pencil on the counter with which to write down the sale of a can of beans or a loaf of bread. No one, not he and certainly not my other brothers, ever knew how much any of the three hundred families in Sundown owed him from month to month, year to year. Until he went broke and crazy, I did not understand his behavior at the counter to have been a symptom of anything but his goodwill, his need to help the poor, the starving, the bereft.

Am I as bereft of direction as my father was? Why do I devote myself to isolation? Writing has been an obsession all my life. Now, garlic has joined the writing.

Vanity, vanity, all is vanity...

Caution. Yellow light. Don't stop to be self-indulgent, like your Poppa. Don't be pretentious...don't try to be a learned philosopher.

Poppa lost everything, went into debt. So could I. So have I.

CHAPTER 16

The Mother of All Maggots Meets the Nematode from Hell

maggot: a worm or grub of the kind formerly supposed to be generated by corruption; chiefly applied to the larva of a dipterous fly. Red maggot: the larva (destructive to corn) of the wheat-midge.

nematode: a microscopic eel-like segmented roundworm. No relation to the earthworm. Roots of most plants in all fifty states are vulnerable to several varieties of nematodes. Beneficial nematodes scorn root crops but attack grubs, root maggots, and cutworms, as well as other nematodes that do attack roots.

"You got onion maggots? Give up tryin' to grow anything in that soil. Pave it over and make it a parking lot. Or maybe just give up farmin' and go to law school."

— A FARMER IN TULARE COUNTY, CALIFORNIA

Whatever obsessions one has—theater playbills, Wedgwood china, Yemeni silver, teak armoires, Spanish tiaras, meerschaum pipes, matchbox covers, playing cards—there is always that one best of breed, which, for some very personal reason, excites its collector's passions more than anything else.

For me, from among my current collection of thirty (thirty-two?) garlics (including Persian Star, France's Rose du Var, Czechoslovakia's Duganskij, Tadzhikistan's Dushanbe), the one garlic that I prize the most (I said *prize*, not *love*) is from Transylvania.

Sebastian Shipke, a Harvard professor in Balkan history (and a collector of ancient Transylvanian erotica) is convinced that Dracula was a cross-dresser. My Transylvanian garlic was blessed by Saint Dracula himself.

I prize my Transylvanian garlic not because of Saint Dracula's attention or because of its special culinary qualities, but because I have struggled so long to force this spirited iconoclastic garlic to bend to my will. It's been thinking about my will, if not bending to it.

As could be expected, the Transylvanian garlic had convinced itself that it was genetically incapable of expatriation. Especially to Occidental, California. Betray Dracula's castle and its medieval lore? Mingle with the *Lumpenproletariat* or other bourgeois *Alliums*? Seek the California sun like a blond, blue-eyed surfer? Any high-caste garlic would, should, smirk at the New World's perpetual sun and sleepy, balmy breezes. The true aristocrat would destroy him-her-itself rather than submit to such a silly master.

Being of Georgian stock, I was well acquainted with the canny instincts that defy all efforts to fight self-destruction. I mothered this garlic, fathered it, nursed it, as I would a sick and tantrumy child.

I succeeded. But at what cost!

The matured Transylvanian head is about the size of a golf ball. It looks like a toy. The cloves, to be seen, require better than 20-20 vision.

For five years I've cursed the Transylvanian garlic as it tried to die. Every clove demanded and received special attention and still ignored nature's demand to reproduce.

Twice, three times, I almost gave up. But I have vowed to protect and cherish my Transylvanian garlic through sickness and health until death (of it or me) do us part.

At the moment things look good. Next June's crop should remove the garlic from its endangered status.

My Transylvanian garlic was a gift from a chance acquaintance, a professor at Brandeis University, a Russian scholar just returned from the Ukraine. On their way home, she and her husband, out of curiosity, had traveled to Transylvania, where, in a shabby market square, she'd purchased ten heads of garlic. It was not difficult to sneak the garlics through customs, she said. She simply wrapped them inside a sanitary napkin.

She'd never thought of eating the little buggers; she only wanted to braid them into a necklace that she would hang on a wall of her office to fend off the hordes of bloodsuckers that populate academia.

I'd met Professor Feur at the home of my friends Margo and Donald Fanger. At dinner Don informed the guests that I was from California and that I grew garlic.

Professor Feur told me about her Transylvanian garlic and I arranged an exchange. I would send her five different varieties of exotic garlics if she would send me a single head from her Transylvanian necklace.

Done.

I hung the single head, appropriately identified, on the rung of one of the clothes dryers serving at the time as an instrument for my curing my relatively small harvest of garlic.

I examined all the various garlics, especially the Transylvanian, daily, to be sure they were not going soft. After all, the temperature inside my solar house is not ideal for storing garlic; warmth and sunlight hasten deterioration.

On the morning of October 15, 1990, I cut the cord on the end of which the single head of Transylvanian garlic had been suspended for two months.

Inside the third thin porcelain sheath were twenty-four cloves. The largest was a shade longer than the nail on my little finger and maybe a millimeter thicker; the smallest, the size of a grain of rice. Compared to the cloves from my Armenian garlic, these Transylvanian cloves were as a whisper of a kitten to the roar of a hungry lion.

I had to taste the garlic, of course, so I ate one clove raw. It proved to be mild, not too hot, but with an extraordinarily intense staying power. I rubbed a second clove, which would have been lost on a whole slice of bread, on a small crouton. Okay, but not impressive.

I planted the remaining twenty-two cloves in a space that would have taken six cloves of Spanish Roja or Creole Red or four cloves of Inchelium Red.

By August 1992, I could see that only three of the twenty-two had survived, offering full heads. The other nineteen had apparently dissolved in the soil.

The three spindly stalks looked as though they would die within hours. Harvested, the heads were only microscopically larger than the original head received from Professor Feur. The pale green, almost-yellow leaves did not stretch up and out to the morning sun but shrank, obviously hoping for shade. Maybe fog. Or a swamp.

Separated in the fall for planting, those three heads produced fifty-four cloves, thirty-one of which were visible and viable enough to be deposited in the soil.

Why, a normal farmer might ask, was I wasting so much time and energy and space to reproduce these puny monsters? I don't know. In the past, when confronted by such failures, I simply stopped working with them, whether they were fuchsias or peaches or cars.

Of the thirty-one cloves planted *that* October, fourteen survived the winter and spring, and gave promise of survival into and through the summer. Then, in the extreme heat of June, six of the fourteen stalks shrank into desiccated corpses.

I forced myself to believe that this generation of eight survivors was visibly more sturdy than its parents or grandparents.

In 1995, I planted ninety-one cloves.

Like the Transylvanian, several of my garlics have come to me as gifts from friends, relatives, chefs, or anonymous travelers.

Four years ago, a friend in Oakland, Sylva Baghdassarian, received three heads of garlic from visiting relatives. It had come from a market in Hadrut Karabakh, a small village once controlled by Azerbaijan but now returned to Armenia. The three heads cost the equivalent of six cents.

Sylva gave me one of those three heads.

Freed of its exterior skin, the head, too large to fit into my open palm, contained nine cloves, each clove longer and thicker than my thumb. I thought at first it might be a head of what is called elephant garlic, but the pungent strength of the Armenian's aroma convinced me it was a true garlic. A mutant, perhaps? A cross between some ancient *Allium sativum* and an albino gorilla?

I shy away from growing too much white garlic because it is generally difficult to peel and does not, for me, have the spectrum of distinct tastes possessed by the red skins. But this white garlic was irresistible. My records show that I planted all nine cloves on October 29, 1992.

Six weeks later, there, in box No. 33, six inches out of the ground, stood, all in a row, nine perfect green spears.

By early February, when the greens of all the other garlics were six to ten inches above ground, the greens of the Armenian garlic reached up to my knees. Each leaf was twice as wide, as heavy, and as thick, as the leaves of any of my other varieties. In appearance alone this garlic promised the durability that could enable it to withstand threats from the most extreme weather or soil or, given its birthplace, centuries (perhaps millennia) of wars and plunder.

Was the early appearance of such healthy greens a result of immediate adaptation to the quality of my soil and to Occidental's climate? Was I on my way perhaps to approximating this garlic's natural environment in distant Armenia?

If it was this impressive now, what on earth would the garlic look like two or three seasons ahead?

I had a probable answer to my question when I harvested the nine garlics and laid them out in the sun for a few minutes on the upturned black soil. They looked like bonsai palm trees just that moment sprung out of basketballs.

I cured the garlic not for two weeks but four.

Out of those first nine heads came seventy cloves. I ate five, so I could compare the garlic to other already-established varieties. I chewed one of the cloves raw. It was moderately hot. In fact, I made a note that the size and promise of this giant was deceptive. Then, suddenly, heat lightning struck at the back of my mouth and dashed up into my sinuses. My eyes filled with tears, and when I tried to talk I thought my vocal cords had been charred. Then, as quickly as it had struck, the heat faded, giving way to a taste that came close, for me, to that of a richly flavored nut. A butternut, perhaps, or a macadamia.

I baked the second clove, and used the third for my very secret and never-to-be-revealed pasta sauce. The fourth went into a salsa. I'd thought of using two cloves here, but the one proved hot and pungent enough to please even the devotees of habanero chilies (the hottest chile in the world). I treated myself, using the fifth clove, with an absolutely supreme bruschetta.

At every step I made notes regarding the comparative qualities of the garlic. I was cautious because I was now considering a competitor to my Russian Red Toch. Well, why not? Armenia and Georgia share a border of perhaps four hundred miles. Armenians and Georgians look alike. How many times have I, in my travels, been asked if I speak Armenian?

I had plans.

In about three years, if all went well, my stock of the Armenian garlic would be more than adequate to allow me to offer this sub-sub-sub-variety of *Allium sativum* to chefs, friends, and anyone else devoted to savoring a food appreciated by a few hundred people in a small village in an almost-inaccessible distant piece of the globe.

If all went well.

It did not.

I'd planted the two distinctly different varieties in neighboring boxes because, I told myself, they deserved each other.

> Rough, tough, coarse Armenian truck-driver garlic seeking tender, fragile, Ophelia-like Transylvanian garlic.
>
> —*Personals*

I harvested the Armenian garlic last year in mid-July, the same week I harvested the latest crop of Transylvanian garlic.

Box No. 17 produced sixty-eight heads of the Armenian. Box No. 18 (which had received 120 cloves of Transylvanian) produced twenty heads.

When I harvested the garlic in boxes No. 16 and 19, on either side of boxes No. 17 and 18, I found more than half of the bulbs infested with worms.

On closer observation of the Armenian garlic through my magnifying glass, I discovered six heads crawling with—not worms, but maggots.

Fifteen of the twenty Transylvanian garlics, which I could not have nursed more lovingly had they been my own children, lay on sheets of plastic like mounds of shimmering Jell-O.

Maggots!

I hurried into the house carrying several of the beasts in my hand. Under my magnifying glass the slimy, snow-white bodies writhed as their legs and pincers sought the dark soil that had nursed them. I wanted to drown the bastards in boiling water. I wanted to hear them scream.

Instead I deposited them in a jar, sealed it, rushed to the Agricultural Department station in Santa Rosa, which is manned by what are called master gardeners, and said, "What do I have?"

The two men and one woman, on hearing I'd discovered them in my garlic beds, gave me a diagnosis. "You have onion maggots."

"You have onion maggots!"

My entire garlic crop—not just a few boxes—was now in danger. Once the remaining maggots completed their cycle and became flies, they could deposit their eggs in every one of my forty boxes.

The master gardeners shook their heads. "There's no known cure for onion maggots," they said.

For the next two weeks, as I harvested the remaining garlic, I found an occasional rotted stalk inhabited by a few gargantuan maggots. In boxes No. 12, 13, and 14 they appeared to be the thighs of woolly mammoths. Snow-white woolly mammoths.

Following Robert's advice, I placed the stalks in a pile and burned them. Not just the contaminated stalks, but every brown leaf, every single stalk or fragment of stalk at hand. I also wiped the blades of all the metal tools I had used so the possible contamination would not be spread to other plants. Robert helped me rake up all straw and paper and soil that could possibly serve as repositories for eggs. We poured gasoline over the mounds and torched everything.

I called various growers of both onions and garlic, in upstate New York, Washington, Oregon, even in Gilroy, where surely the latest knowledge about garlic predators had to be available.

The universal response: generous clucks of tongues, as if I'd just recited my own obituary.

Only Salvatore Danofrio in Gilroy offered empathy. I'd met Salvatore in my trips to Gilroy a few years ago. He remembered me, and said he'd read about me in the papers. Pretending outrage, he shouted that I was running him out of the business. A tough but wily old wizard, Salvatore and his sons and daughters farm two thousand acres of garlic (California Late, California Early) on the outskirts of Gilroy. He employs a hundred workers. He knows almost as much about garlic as Dracula. He also knows that, concerning the sale of garlic, I'm no threat.

"You grow your garlic in boxes, I remember, right?"

"That's right, Sal."

"You got onion maggots. *E peccato.* Take my advice. Next four years, you don't grow garlic in any the boxes they got maggots. Shovel out the soil. Spray. Spray everything. Turn the soil over three, four times. Keep spraying. Spray the boxes, spray the wire bottoms, spray the ground under the wire. Use the worst stuff the government still allows you to use."

"Spray? Toxic spray?"

"No other way. One thing. You're sure they're *onion* maggots? There's all kinds of maggots, you know."

"Sal, they are monstrous big. The size of a tank. Three master gardeners at the Ag. Department told me they were onion maggots."

"That means they're probably not. Those guys they look at the maggots under a microscope?"

"No. They eyeballed them."

"Well, most master gardeners, whatever the hell that means, never seen an onion maggot. You do anything different last year?"

"I brought in fresh goat manure."

"You put it on fresh?"

"I'm afraid I did, Sal."

"*Stupido. Molto stupido.* Well, I'll talk to someone. My son Tony. He's going to school. U.C. Davis. He's gonna run this business when I retire.

I'll tell him to call you. Don't take chances, though. Go to church. Try praying to the Holy Mother. What's your number?"

"What's Her number, Sal?"

"Hey, that's good."

Anthony Danofrio called that night. "Dad told me you might have onion maggots."

"Not me, my garlic."

"He said you were funny. You know about nematodes? They eat maggots."

"No. Are you being funny now? What are nematodes?"

"They're microscopic organisms that attack the roots of plants."

"But you said they eat maggots."

"The good nematodes do that, too."

"You think I have bad nematodes as well as onion maggots?"

"Oh, I'm sure there are nematodes in your soil. All the soil in all fifty states has nematodes. But there are bad nematodes and good nematodes. Bad guys and good guys. Villains and heroes. Black hats and white hats."

"You ought to change your major from Agriculture to English, Anthony. You have a flair for words."

"No, thanks. Well, I do read books. Look, I'm working for a company called biosys, in Palo Alto. Summer intern. Biosys is commercializing effective bioinsecticides based on nematodes. On beneficial nematodes."

"Good guys. Heroes. The todes with the white hats."

"You got it. Anyway, biosys produces beneficial nematodes and farmers and gardeners buy them to eat the bad nematodes in their soil. Not too many people realize these good nematodes also eat insect larvae. That's the maggot before it becomes a fly."

"Wait a minute. What the hell's a bioinsecticide?"

"It's a biological alternative to a chemical insecticide. At biosys, it's based on the use of nematodes. Doesn't pollute the soil or harm the crop. Totally ecologically safe. The EPA supports it. The product biosys produces is sold in your area at Harmony Farm Supply in Sebastopol."

"Ten minutes from where I live."

"That's what I figured. I looked at a map. You want to talk to someone here at biosys who knows a hell of a lot more than I do. Here's a number to call."

Seconds after Anthony hung up I called Stephen Manweiler. He is an entomologist at biosys.

He was to be my guide through hell.

It is true that there is no known antidote for onion maggots, and biosys certainly did not suggest that their nematodes be relied on as such a weapon. But what if the maggots had not been identified correctly? What if my maggots were one of the thirteen species of *Steinernema* or one of the four species of *Heterorhabditis* that the good nematodes consume? Not just consume, but actually require for their own brief flight through their own maggoty cosmos?

I'd lose nothing by trying the nematodes.

"I'll send you some articles," Stephen promised.

I received the articles three days after we talked. In reciprocity (he'd mentioned his being a gardener and being interested in drip irrigation), I sent him a copy of Robert's *Edible Landscape* and *Drip Irrigation*.

The text of most of the articles I received from Stephen was fairly heavy for a writer/professor/farmer, but there was enough that, translated into my native tongue, served to impress and depress me, edging me into the personality disorder termed *Schizophrenia agricultura*.

> Both *Steinernema* and *Heterorhabditis* pass through four juvenile stages before maturing. Only the third-stage juvenile (infective or dauer) can survive outside an insect host and move from one insect to another. Infective juveniles carry in their intestines symbiotic bacteria (*Xenorhabdus s* pp.) that they release after entering the insect haemocoel by way of natural openings (spiracles, mouth, anus) and, in the case of *Heterorhabditis*, directly through the cuticle of certain insects (Bedding and Molyneux, 1982). The *Xenorhabdus* cells proliferate, kill the insect host (usually in 24-72 hours) and render its interior favorable for nematode development. The entering infectives develop into hermaphroditic females (*Heterorhabditis*) or males and females (*Steinernema*). One or more generation of progeny develop, reproduction continuing

> until host-derived nutrients are depleted. At this time the nematodes synchronously become third-stage juvenile infectives that leave the cadaver to search for new hosts by detecting insect excretory products, carbon dioxide emissions and...
>
> *Agricultural Zoology Reviews, vol. 6, October 1994*
>
> —R. Georgis and S. A. Manweiler

I bought a container of biosys nematodes at Harmony Farm Supply in Sebastopol and, at home, read the directions on the label to be sure I was proceeding correctly.

I thoroughly soaked the soil in the boxes I knew to be contaminated. They had been noted in my journal.

I opened the container, which was filled to the lip with tiny brown balls composed of what looked like clay.

Eight tablespoons of the good little clay babies, as advised (two spoons for each gallon), went into my four-gallon sprinkling can. After adding three gallons of water, I waited for one minute and stirred for exactly thirty seconds. I filled the can with water, stirred the mix for exactly sixty seconds, and sprinkled the mix (millions of hungry little nematodes) on the surface of the soaked soil in each contaminated box. Then I set the sprinklers for another ten minutes to soak the good todes deeper.

The work took me into the evening. The following three days, as the instructions demanded, I again watered each of those boxes in which the nematodes were feasting. I hoped.

At the moment, the garlic in every box (including the Transylvanian and the Armenian) looks fine.

I'll know in two to three months whether or not I should shoot myself, torch all the boxes, or just simply dine on maggot salad for the next twenty-four years.

If the nematodes work, I'm buying stock in biosys.

Chapter 17

Tales from the Garlicky Crypt

GARLIC FOR TOOTHACHE

I've suffered toothaches twice in my life. Except for earache, nothing else so certifies the existence of Satan.

My first experience was when I was about ten.

I woke up screaming at midnight.

Over the next several hours, my mother and father tried every known home remedy.

First: oil of clove, kept on hand for my brother's earaches. My mother, as she reached into my mouth to locate the villainous tooth, cooed to me in Polish, in German, in Yiddish. English had no power to soothe the savage beast. My tooth continued to punish me terribly, but it seemed I was now able to better hear the higher registers of my own screams.

Next: my father wrapped a hot iron in a moist towel and placed the package against the offending cheek. That triangular patch on my cheek has remained smooth and hairless ever since. That night it felt like being jabbed with a twenty-pronged pitchfork deep into my jawbone.

Then (it must now have been four in the morning) my father poured some of his homemade dandelion wine onto a piece of none-to-clean cotton and daubed and jabbed at the tooth for several minutes. The taste of foul, dusty wine helped not at all.

Finally (near sunrise?), my father, who was smoking two or more packs of Lucky Strike cigarettes a day, removed two cigarettes from a near-empty pack. He tore one cigarette apart. Using the head of a match he packed the tobacco onto, into, around, the tooth. Within minutes the pain began to fade.

We all relaxed.

Ten minutes later I was sound asleep.

An hour later I leaped awake, screaming. My father, partly in frustration but partly because it was a natural progression of cultural momentum, said, "I know. I tell you, I know."

He went to the cupboard where he stored his precious garlic, removed one clove, peeled it, cut it in half, and ignoring my groans and grunts, pressed the exposed side onto my tooth. I was gagging as he manipulated his fingers and fist inside my mouth, but he would not have stopped had I swallowed his arm up to his shoulder.

Un miracolo!

Ol' devil was defeated.

I slept like the baby I was until that afternoon when, without the slightest pain in my jaw, I walked to town to Dr. Shapiro's office.

Dr. Shapiro tilted me back in his leather chair, opened my mouth and almost fell over backwards. "You," Dr. Shapiro said, wiping his eyes, "have terrible breath. Don't you ever brush your teeth? That's your problem! Brush your teeth, for God's sake! Twice a day! Especially before you come to my office."

Three weeks ago—some sixty-two years later—I woke up screaming. At least I woke up trying to scream. At least I woke up. Seventy-two-year-old men no longer have the voicebox for the production of screams much beyond the growl of a basenji.

My molar—bottom, right side—was on fire.

I remembered Poppa.

I made it downstairs, dug about in my garlic pot, found a clove of appropriate size (Achatami from Soviet Georgia—forgive me, Alexei, the Republic of Georgia), peeled it, cut it, and held the cut side in place. In five minutes the pain was gone. I went to bed with the clove ensconced. Sometime during the night I must have chomped it to bits and swallowed it. I woke up at six with both garlic and toothache gone.

I learn. Not necessarily fast but eventually. Before I went to the dentist in Berkeley I brushed my teeth and gargled Listerine. It didn't help.

Dr. Olesen said, “Lord, Chester, you have terrible breath. Go in the bathroom and brush your teeth or I can’t work on you.”

I explained everything but he appeared skeptical. He probably thought I was just another senile old geezer who, beside never brushing his teeth probably also never changed his underwear.

The old filling was removed and a new one set in place in thirty minutes. Since then I’ve had not a moment of pain.

GARLIC FOR LOWER GUT PAIN

For several years, before I began my teaching career at Saint Mary’s College, I was an X-ray technician.

I’d trained at Cowell Hospital on the Berkeley campus of the University of California. After I passed my registry exam I worked in San Francisco at Kaiser Hospital.

One night I was on call, meaning I would be called should emergency X-rays be required after the department closed at six o’clock.

I came home to Berkeley after my regular shift, had supper with my wife and son, and received my first call about eight o’clock. A patient, the switchboard operator informed me, was being brought in by ambulance. An eighty-two-year old man with severe abdominal pains. The physician had requested an exploratory film, a flat plate of the abdomen, to rule out appendicitis. He obviously was not aware that too often a single film of the abdomen does not by itself verify a ruptured appendix. Regardless, I would, as the doctor requested, phone him when I was preparing to take the film. He would meet me, I was told, in the X-ray department.

I raced across the Bay Bridge and arrived in the Kaiser Radiology department in time to spread a warm sheet on the cold table just before the ambulance arrived. The driver helped me shift Mr. Stanley Kovacz from the gurney onto the cotton sheet spread across the table. After I covered the patient with two more warm sheets, the driver helped me remove his shoes and trousers and shirt.

Mr. Kovacz was wearing old-fashioned BVDs. I would have to remove them because the buttons could block important anatomy or even give false shadows on the film.

It was a struggle.

Mr. Kovacz could not speak English, but with what had to be curses and weak swings of both arms and legs he let us know he would not have his BVDs removed. Rather than create more distress, I decided to leave the underwear in place. If the buttons proved to be a problem I'd take a second film.

The ambulance driver had other things to do and left me alone with Mr. Kovacz, but before he left he helped me strap the patient to the table.

I tried to ask relevant questions ("Where's the pain?" "Did you fall?" "Can you hold your breath when I ask you to?"), but the patient did not understand me. The admissions nurse, Inge Neilsen, coming into the room to band his wrist, tried to help me but gave up sooner than I did. "The admissions form says he's Hungarian," Mrs. Neilsen said. "I'll try to find someone in the house who speaks the language. If it was Danish we'd have no problem."

I called the doctor and said I was about to take the film. It would be out of the darkroom in about ten minutes. I prepared the equipment and, as requested, exposed a single film, not even trying to direct Mr. Kovacz to hold his breath but observing his chest through the leaded glass window. I caught him on what I hoped was a full exhalation.

In the darkroom, after the exposed film went into the automatic processor, I slipped a new film into the cassette. I'd probably have to take that second film because the odds were that Mr. Kovacz had breathed or moved during the first film.

Ten minutes later, when the film came out of the automatic processor, I hung it on the fluorescent panel and said to myself, "What the hell is that?" just as the doctor, who'd finally arrived, said, "What the hell is that?"

"That," I said, "must be something on the table."

"Didn't you check?"

"I didn't see it when I undressed him. I had him practically naked. There wasn't anything under him. I'll check him again and take another film."

Back at the table, taking Mr. Kovacz's punches on my head and shoulders, I felt beneath his rump, beneath his thighs, between his thighs, inside his BVDs. Nothing. I think the term he kept throwing at me in what I presumed to be Hungarian meant *pervert*. The doctor, who'd stood at my side the whole time, also checked the table as well as Mr. Kovacz's body. He was apparently, in the patient's mind, a graduate pervert, as the Hungarian term had an extra syllable or two.

The doctor and I returned to the viewing box.

"Something's sticking out of his anus," the doctor said. "I could actually feel something."

"Congratulations. You were a bit more forward than I was. Yes, I can see now that something is definitely sticking out of his anus. It looks like a bunch of chopsticks. No, too thick for chopsticks. And too short."

"I'll ask him," the doctor said.

"Do you speak Hungarian?"

"No."

"Then don't bother asking. Mrs. Neilsen's trying to find…and speaking of the devil…"

Inge Neilsen appeared, followed by a short, chunky woman wearing a nurse's-aide uniform. The whites of her eyes looked as if they'd been injected with muddy water.

"Miss Horensky speaks Hungarian," Inge said.

"Miss Horensky," the doctor said, "would you please ask the patient if he knows what's protruding from his anus."

She tried to process the words and finally managed to repeat a fair number of them in English in almost logical order. She left and, a few minutes later, reappeared. She'd been restraining herself but here, in the viewing area, she exploded. Laughing in Hungarian requires a great deal of rib clutching and deep inhalation.

Finally, sufficiently sobered to speak, Miss Kortenshy, as the doctor called her, said, "Sorry. You not believe. Patient hear clove garlic good for…um…how you say hemorrhoid, Hungarian?"

"Hemorrhoid?" the doctor repeated.

"Well, one clove good hemorrhoid, whole head better. So he stuff two whole head up ass. I think maybe he leave leaves. I go look see."

She left, came back. "He leave leaves also too."

"Thank you, Miss Kortenshy. Miss Neilsen, would you call O.R. Tell them I have a hot appendix on an eighty-five-year-old male with high blood pressure. They better prepare for surgery. I'll have to call a surgeon. The poor bastard hasn't had a bowel movement for seventy-two hours. That explains his gut ache."

"The surgeon?"

Inge burst out laughing, then recovered, then succeeded in looking very sad. "*Pobrecito*," she said. Why she didn't use the Danish word I never asked.

Note, please: Mr. Kovacz survived.

He's probably still alive, still eating garlic. And still using it for everything from psoriasis to halitosis. The doctor? Dead. About twelve years ago. I'm betting he hadn't eaten more than three garlic cloves in his entire life.

GHOSTS, THE DEVIL, WEREWOLVES, AND PSYCHIC REVELATIONS

I have a neighbor here in Occidental named Sage. She has a very impressionable daughter named Antonia. Tony. Tony is in her second year in high school.

Tony is considered strange even by her peers. Sons and daughters of well-intentioned and now middle-class former hippies, these kids hang out in front of the grocery store in downtown Occidental trying to look and act big city, speaking rapper-ese.

Tony communes with the spirit world. Her peers indulge her, her parents aren't too concerned about her because they, now in their late forties, remember too well their own conviction before her birth that they would change the world. If not the world, the U.S. If not the U.S., California. If not the state, then San Francisco. Now they raise goats in Occidental.

When the winds are right, or wrong, on hot afternoons, I can smell goat shit. This is not one of the prime pleasures in life.

Invited to one of their suppers, I await that moment when, instead of saying grace, we hold hands and call "ooooom" as we breathe in, "ahmmmm" when we breathe out. And add, for thirty seconds, the incantation: "Peace...love...peace...love..."

Then everyone rips into the pork chops.

About a year ago, at two o'clock in the morning, Sage pounded on my door. I jumped out of bed and pulled on a robe. Sage stood in the porch light looking like a banshee. "Garlic! Lots of it. Heads. Fifteen or twenty."

I didn't ask why. Who does in such a situation? But I did grab my flashlight and, after stopping in my curing shed to fill a bag with garlic, I accompanied Sage through the darkness back across the fields to her home. On the way she enlightened me.

"Tony's been acting weird, man. For weeks now. Months. I think she's having a spiritual crisis. She moans and cries out when she's sleeping. Tonight, a half hour ago, she started screaming. It was terrible. Whitman and I ran in and found her thrashing about in the bed. There were two bites, on her neck. Oozing blood. The window was wide open. The wind was just terrible. And the room ...well, it just smelled bad, man. Like a ...a crypt."

"What the hell are you saying? You think she was bitten by a vampire?"

"I know it. I just know it. It had to be a vampire."

She was correct about the window being open and there was indeed a fetid aroma in the room and there certainly was blood on the pillow and Tony sure as hell had marks on her throat and, yes, her eyes were still glazed.

I didn't object when Sage and Whitman scurried about laying heads of garlic on window sills and under Tony's pillows and even stringing a head (Red Tempest from Formosa) around her throat.

"It might have been a raccoon," I said. "Or a feral cat. You better take her to a doctor tomorrow. You know, raccoons and cats can carry rabies."

"Are you kidding? With our two dogs out there? There haven't been cats or raccoons around the place since we moved in."

Well, the garlic worked. Tony recovered from the vampire bites.

But the garlic did not succeed as well as a contraceptive would have. Tony gave birth to a beautiful son with dark hair and light-blue eyes.

Sage and Whitman still hang garlic all over the house. Even under Tony's pillow.

Chapter 18

I Stomp the Wineglass

Thanksgiving day is cold. With heavy winds.

Rain, the weather station has reported, is likely north of San Francisco. Meaning here in Occidental. For once the weather reporters are correct.

Mary Catherine O'Connor and Siobhan, her daughter, and Oona, her granddaughter, arrive mid afternoon for supper. They will stay over tonight and drive home tomorrow, after lunch.

Oona talks for two hours after supper, after we consume all but one slice of Mary Catherine's mince-meat pie, about sleeping in front of the fire, about the possibility of sharing her sleeping bag with Sadie.

I check her for ticks (Sadie, not Oona), which can be a nuisance in the late autumn. Sadie is clean.

We sit in front of the iron stove, soaking up the heat from the crackling madrona logs. We're drinking John Jamison. Oona sips hot chocolate to which her grandmother, with the acquiescence of Oona's mother, has added four drops of the Jamison. I am the designated consumer of the final slice of pie.

"Now, Mommy?" Oona asks, after I return the cleaned plate to the sink.

Siobhan nods her head.

Oona produces from behind several folds of blue skirt and purple turtleneck a blank envelope wrapped with red ribbon. She delivers it to me with a very serious face, as if she is about to demand something non-negotiable.

I open the letter, expecting a Season's Greeting, a piece of lined classroom paper covered with a drawing, by Oona, of a fat turkey.

It is a piece of paper allright. But it is a letter with the embossed imprint of a publisher. An editor is interested in publishing my book.

The ensuing celebration depletes the John Jamison, so I produce a bottle of Manischewitz.

"No," both women gasp. Oona, dutifully influenced, adds her own high-soprano chirp.

"A tiny glass for each," I insist. "It's called a *bissel warmt*. I've had this wine for ten years."

"No worry," Mary Catherine assures me. "Sugar preserves grape syrup for a century."

We down the stuff as if it is Malt Scotch. Which it is. Kosher Malt Scotch.

"Do you have an agent?" Siobhan manages to push the five words through gritting and grinding teeth.

"No."

"I'll find you an agent. Man or woman?"

"A woman. My fate, like my body, is more secure in the hands of a woman."

"I know someone."

Mary Catherine is blinking hard, trying to convince herself she is too tough to be moved by such triumphs. And she's certainly not surprised. Hadn't she been convinced of my eventual good fortune ever since we'd first met?

When I kneel at her chair to thank her, Mary Catherine grins, the model for one of those country lassies in an Aire Lingus commercial, all clean, pink skin and big, blue-green eyes. Even though it would be stretching two points to call her a colleen.

"Is Chester going to propose to Grandma?" Oona asks.

Siobhan rolls her eyes. "Is Oona going to hold her little pink tongue?"

"Oona, come over here, please."

She comes to me, so confident, so trusting, so innocent, I yearn to embrace her forever. What must I do to protect the child from the world she'll be inheriting?

"Yes," I say. "Chester is going to propose to your grandma."

Oona pushes herself free, crosses the room to Mary Catherine, who is now wiping her eyes. Oona waits, curious, and, I want to believe, hopeful.

I get down on my knees.

"Is that how it's done?" Oona asks not me but her mother.

"Oona, come over here by your doting mother."

"Before you go," Mary Catherine whispers into Oona's ear, "Tell the man your grandma accepts his proposal. It's the best one I've had all day."

I ask Mary Catherine when we should tie the knot. Should it be formal? In a church? Which one? Soon? Will we have a party?

She looks for a moment as if I've lost it, as if I am beyond hope. She laughs her songbird trill and makes a sound that sounds like *huch!* but which, she says, is Gaelic for *yes*. "Church," she says. "Or here. Or your place in Occidental. Or the county dump. Doesn't matter."

"Yes, in Russian," I say, "is *da* ."

"In Dublin ... Dou-blen...da means father, daddy, poppa ... pa." She nods and says *huch!* once more, but this time with what Italians call *spirito* . Energy. Spirit. And with tears. *Con lacrimae.*

"I have to call Siobhan," she sniffles, lifting the phone. "Have to know what's a good date for her."

"I'm not marrying Siobhan. Do you know what time it is in New York?"

"The same time as here in California," she says, "only three hours later."

A late summer wedding.

There is a canopy.

An orthodox rabbi and an unorthodox priest have agreed to co-sponsor this union.

At noon, priest and rabbi link arms and cheer as I stomp the napkin-wrapped wineglass. The rabbi drinks (from a different glass) and offers his glass, containing wine, to the priest.

Father Corrigan does not drink. "Never touch the stuff."

Father's wink is labored. Then, probably fearing retribution from on-high or below, Father Corrigan accepts the glass from Rabbi Weisman and sips. And sips again. And sips a third time.

The rabbi is patient but even rabbis have limited endurance. "Nu?" the Rabbi whispers, in a not very guarded aside.

I've invited twelve relatives and all my friends, including the entire Albini family. I'm pleased to see Kelli and Brenda walk through the crowd together, holding hands. Louis and Susan and the grandchildren are all here now also, along with forty or fifty others—just about all of whom are relatives of Mary Catherine's.

Mary Catherine's aunts rely on the rhythm method. "Vatican roulette," she calls it. Consequence(s): there are so many Michaels and Pauls and Marys I jump as if jabbed, at the call behind my back, "Natey, come taste this hummus," and "Rachel, this polenta is to die for."

And Isaac.

"Isaac?" Oona Daugherty asks. "What kind of name is that?"

"That," Mary Catherine lectures her granddaughter, "is a name out of the Old Testament. You'll read it some day."

Father Corrigan rolls his eyes and shakes an advisory (threatening?) finger at daughter and mother.

On the long, orange table, shaded by the leaves of the Perlette Seedless grapes, the Red Flame grapes and the Concord Blues, among the platters of garlic dishes, in bowls and baskets: my Asian pears (only the Hosuis); my peaches (Strawberry, Red Nectar, Indian Blood); my plumcots (Luther Burbank); my plums (Santa Rosa, Elephant Heart, American President, Greengage); my apples (Gravenstein, Fameuze, Macintosh, Spitzenberg, yellow and red delicious, pippin—too bad the Arkansas Blacks will not be ready for three months); my domestic pears (Bartlett, Bosc, Sekel); and my cherries (Queen Anne only, the bings having been eaten by birds months ago).

My mother's fruits.

I even kiss Patrick Earl O'Connor, Mary Catherine's paddy-daddy (her term).

"If you tried this on a Friday night in my old precinct," Patrick Earl O'Connor advises me, "I or my friends would do you serious injury. Welcome to an honest family. Now wait a minute." He looks to his daughter.

"What's the word I'm supposed to say here, Mary Catherine?"

"Simcha," she tells him, pronouncing it perfectly. After all, she's studied Gaelic.

"I can't pronounce that."

"You can, Daddy. Simcha. Say it."

"Simka. I can't gargle like my daughter but I tried. It's a blessing, right? OK. I said it. Now I can run for Mayor of Dublin."

I turn to Louis. "Boychik, let's eat!"

It is October. Time to plant.

Mary Catherine has tied up her red hair in a blue bandanna. She is wearing shorts and sneakers. The Irish skin, when it does take a tan, has that almost rusty glow of my evening skies. Such is Mary Catherine's skin now. She has worked in the sun every day for a month of her summer vacation. She has set her own traps and caught two gophers.

Lordy, what a life!

What I wouldn't give to have Momma and Poppa here to work with Mary Catherine and me as we very tenderly place each clove in its private womb.

But they are here.

They sit with us on our deck every evening, watching the deer grazing the meadow in the light that floats in from the sea like molten gold.

"Boychik, you did it. You did what I couldn't do. You made a business and you made a profit."

My mother, in Polish, my father, in Russian, murmur over and over to themselves, to each other, to Mary Catherine, to me: "Such a golden land."

My mother, that dark, doe-eyed beauty, sings in six languages every evening except Friday, when, only in Hebrew, she prays, reminding God of her desolate past but thanking Him for reaching down to deposit on me, her baby, this woman, this land, this life.

In the darkness, Momma's prayers float in the air like the songs of hovering nightingales.

Listen.

Recipes

MOST OF THE DISHES THAT FOLLOW are moderate to high in calories, but remember that garlic is said to lower blood pressure. Do you want to live to eat or eat to live? Make your choice.

SAUCES, DRESSINGS, AND APPETIZERS

Garlic Oil

Fill a 1-pint jar with olive oil and add 10 minced garlic cloves. Let sit at room temperature for 3 days. Strain through a fine-meshed sieve. Reserve the garlic, place it in a tightly sealed jar, and refrigerate.

The oil can, if desired, be decanted into a bottle. It can remain at room temperature for 1 week. After 1 week, refrigerate the oil for up to 3 weeks. Four to 5 hours before using, let the oil come to room temperature.

The reserved garlic can be used in salads, pasta sauces, glazes, stuffings, stews, or on bruschetta.

Roasted Garlic

To roast single cloves: Preheat the oven to 375°. Remove largest and/or fattest cloves from a head or heads of garlic. Cut the tips from each clove. Do not be concerned if some of the cloves lose their skin. Place the cloves on a piece of flat aluminum foil. Drizzle the cloves with olive oil, then sprinkle them with salt and pepper. Fold the foil to enclose the cloves in a loose but secure packet. Place on a baking sheet and bake on the middle rack of the oven for 45 minutes. Let cool, unfold the foil, and serve.

To roast whole heads: Preheat the oven to 375°. Remove the outer layers of the skins, but try to avoid separating the individual cloves. With a very sharp knife, cut the cap head off so that the tips of every clove are removed. Drizzle the entire head with oil. Bake in a small pan, uncovered, for 45 minutes.

Ai, Aïoli

6 to 10 cloves Burgundy garlic, roasted (see page 179)

1 large or 2 small eggs

1¼ cups olive oil

Juice of ½ lemon

—Makes 1½ cups

Put the garlic cloves and egg(s) in a blender. Blend at low speed to form a paste. With the blender running, trickle in the olive oil. Add the lemon juice to mix. If the aïoli separates, let it sit for a few minutes, then stir. If it is still curdled, add the juice of the remaining lemon half.

Chester's Galaxy-Famous Bruschetta

2 slices white bread, preferably saltless

1 or 2 large French Red Hanan or Acropolis Red garlic cloves, halved

2 or 4 tablespoons extra virgin olive oil

Salt and pepper to taste

—Serves 1

Grill or toast the bread, which should have a firm crust and a dense texture so the bread won't tear when rubbed with garlic. Do not char the bread. Rub the cut side of the garlic cloves on both sides of the still-warm bread. Pour 1 tablespoon of oil on one side of each slice of the bread. Sprinkle with salt and pepper.

Variation: for a spring lunch, top bruschetta with slices of fresh tomato, fresh basil leaves, and coarsely grated Parmegiano-Reggiano cheese.

Test box of eight different varieties. I only kept two for seed.

Display of the varieties used in the 1992 Occidental garlic taste-off.

Sadie

Hadley Salz's Dip

12 Dukanskij garlic cloves, roasted (see page 179)

½ cup finely chopped onion

¼ habanero chile, minced

2 tablespoons olive oil

3 cups refried pinto beans

3 large tomatoes, peeled and chopped

¾ cup warm water

2 teaspoons light molasses

3 tablespoons fresh lemon or lime juice

Salt to taste

¾ cup (3 ounces) grated cheese

— Makes 5 cups

Sauté the garlic, onion, and chile in oil. Stir in all the other ingredients except the cheese. Simmer for 15 minutes. Add more water if necessary. Taste and adjust the seasonings. Stir in the cheese and serve.

The Devil's Sauce

2 bell peppers, seeded, deveined, and coarsely chopped

2 jalapeño chiles, seeded, or ¼ habanero chile, seeded

1 cup coarsely chopped onion

3 tablespoons cider vinegar

2 tablespoons extra virgin olive oil

2 tablespoons sugar

1 teaspoon ground cumin

4 tablespoons red pepper flakes

10 Romanian Red garlic cloves, roasted (see page 179)

1½ teaspoons salt

¼ teaspoon pepper

—Makes 2 cups.

Place the bell peppers, chiles, and onion in a blender or food processor and process to a coarse purée. Pour into a medium saucepan and add the vinegar, oil, sugar, cumin, and pepper flakes. Simmer over low heat for 5 minutes. Add roasted garlic and simmer for 5 minutes. Let cool. Store in the refrigerator in an airtight container for up to 3 weeks or freeze for up to 3 months.

Sardines con Amore

2 cans sardines, preferably in oil

6 ounces cream cheese, at room temperature

¼ cup olive oil

Salt and pepper to taste

12 Romanian Red garlic cloves, roasted (see page 179)

2 teaspoons mayonnaise

¼ teaspoon sweet, store-bought mustard

6-8 slices rye bread (depending on size)

— SERVES 4

Place the sardines, cream cheese, oil, salt, and pepper in a blender or food processor and purée. In a small bowl, mix the mayonnaise, mustard, and roasted garlic. Spread the rye bread with the sardine spread. Top each with a dollop of the garlic mixture.

Garlic Pesto with Olive Spread

8 Spanish Roja garlic cloves, minced

1 bunch fresh parsley

4 ounces pine nuts

A dash of olive oil

8 ounces cream cheese, at room temperature

1 small can sliced black olives, drained

1 bunch fresh basil, stemmed

— MAKES 2 CUPS

Put the garlic, parsley, pine nuts, and olive oil in a blender or food processor and chop. In a medium bowl, mix the remaining ingredients and add it to the mixture. Store, covered, in the refrigerator for up to 1 week.

Russian Black Eyes Appetizers

12 hard-boiled egg yolks

2 tablespoons mayonnaise

1 tablespoon olive oil

Salt and pepper to taste

8 Georgian Crystal garlic cloves,roasted (see page 179)

Crackers

1 small can sliced black olives, drained

Anchovy paste

— SERVES 6

Place the egg yolks, mayonnaise, oil, salt, pepper, and garlic in a blender or food processor. Spread on crackers and top each with a ribbon of anchovy paste. Press 1 olive slice into the anchovy paste.

Eggplant-Garlic Appetizer

1 cup extra virgin olive oil

5 Metechi garlic heads

3 medium eggplants, halved lengthwise

— SERVES 6

Preheat the oven to 350°F.

Pour the oil on a baking sheet with sides or in a shallow baking pan. Arrange the garlic slices on the sheet or pan in the shapes of the eggplant halves. Rub the eggplant halves with oil and place them, cut side down, on top of the garlic slices. Bake for 45 to 60 minutes, or until the skins begin to shrivel. Turn off the oven and let cool to room temperature.

Serving Suggestion: smear the garlic and eggplant pulp on thin toast or crackers.

SOUPS AND BREADS

Cream of Garlic Soup

2 tablespoons butter

⅔ cup sliced French Red shallots

¾ pound baby lima beans

2 cups chopped, cooked chicken

½ teaspoon salt

1 small jalapeño chile, seeded and chopped

¼ teaspoon dried marjoram

6 fresh flat-leaf parsley

½ cup milk or cream

2½ cups homemade chicken or canned low-salt chicken broth

8 Yugoslavian Red garlic cloves, roasted (see page 179)

Snipped fresh chives, for garnish

— Serves 6 to 8

Melt the butter in a large skillet and add the shallots. Cover and cook on low heat for 15 minutes.

In a blender or food processor, combine the beans, shallot mixture, chicken, salt, chile, marjoram, garlic, and parsley. Process at high speed for 20 seconds. With the motor running, gradually add the milk or cream. Pour mixture into a saucepan. Add the broth. Cook over low heat for 10 minutes. Serve hot.

New-Fashioned Vegetable Soup

1 beef knucklebone, cracked

8 cups water

3 tablespoons olive oil

3 pounds beef stew meat, cut into 1-inch cubes

One 20-ounce can whole tomatoes, chopped

14 Inchelium Red garlic cloves, roasted (see page 179)

1 tablespoon salt

1 large jalapeño chile, seeded and chopped

1 large bay leaf

½ teaspoon dried thyme

½ teaspoon dried rosemary

4 fresh flat-leaf parsley sprigs

2 cups diced celery

2 cups diced carrots, peeled

2 cups chopped red cabbage

½ cup diced turnip or rutabaga, peeled

½ cup diced parsnip

1 potato, diced

1 tablespoon unsalted butter

2 cups chopped French Red shallots

10 ounces green beans

10 ounces baby lima beans

10 ounces corn kernels

— Serves 8 to 10

Preheat the oven to 400°F.

Place the knucklebone in a roasting pan and bake for 1 hour, turning the bone every 20 minutes.

Pour the water into a large stockpot and place over high heat. In a large skillet over medium heat, heat the olive oil and brown the beef on all sides. When the water starts boiling, add the roasted knucklebone, browned beef cubes, tomatoes, garlic, and salt. Reduce heat to medium. Add the chile, bay leaf, thyme, rosemary, and parsley. Simmer for 10 minutes. Add the celery, carrots, cabbage, turnip, parsnip, and potato. Simmer for 10 minutes.

In a small skillet over medium heat, melt the butter. Add the shallots, cover, and cook for 10 minutes. Add the shallots to the soup. Add the green beans, lima beans, and corn. Bring to a boil for 10 minutes. Remove the knucklebone, and skim the surface to remove fat and foam. Cover the soup and boil for 20 minutes. Serve very hot.

Very Quick Green Garlic Soup

1 pound steamed green peas, green beans, or broccoli

8 to 12 Purple Tip garlic cloves

1 pound red potatoes, peeled and boiled till tender

6 cups rich chicken stock

Salt and pepper to taste

—SERVES 4 TO 5

Put the green vegetables in a blender with the garlic. Blend. Add the potatoes and blend. Add the stock, salt and pepper. Blend at high speed. Stir and serve.

This soup reheats well. If you want creamier soup, add ½ cup warm half-and-half. To intensify the green color, blend in a handful of chopped fresh flat-leaf parsley. Add potatoes to thicken, or stock to thin.

Chester's Garlic-Sage Soup

2 large Texas Granta onions, sliced

1 teaspoon butter

20 Creole Red garlic cloves, chopped or minced

Salt and pepper to taste

6 small Yukon Gold potatoes, peeled and diced

3 cups water

8 cups beef stock

½ to 1 cup milk or cream

1 cup fresh lemon sage leaves, chopped

½ cup chopped, fresh, flat-leaf parsley

— SERVES 4

In a small skillet, sauté the onions in the butter. Add the garlic, and sauté for 5 minutes. Add salt and pepper. Transfer to a food processor, add the remaining ingredients, and purée, adding warm water as necessary.

Two of the following bread recipes won a gold medal and a silver medal, respectively, at the 1995 Sonoma County Harvest Fair. They were made by my neighbors Renee Des Georges and Eric Dahlquist. Eric was the head chef at Harmony Bakery in Palo Alto, where he won the first place in the *Bay Foods* bread contest.

Eric recommends using organic flour. He uses flour from Giusto's Vitagrains in South San Francisco, which is available at most natural food stores in Northern California.

Soudough Starter

4½ cups water

5 pounds unwashed organic fruit

1 teaspoon salt

12 cups flour

— MAKES APPROXIMATELY 12 CUPS (5 POUNDS)

Put the water in a large bowl. Obtain the bacteria for fermenting the dough by washing each of the fruits, one at a time, in the water. Filter the water through a coffee filter into a large bowl of a heavy-duty mixer. Whisk in the salt and ½ cup of the flour at a time. Switch to a wooden spoon when the dough becomes stiff.

Fit the mixer with a dough hook, and knead for 3-5 minutes. Or, knead by hand on a lightly floured surface for 20-30 minutes, or until smooth, dusting the surface with more flour, 1 tablespoon at a time, as necessary to keep the dough from sticking. Place the dough in a large plastic bag, seal, and let sit at room temperature for 4-5 days.

You are now ready to make Sour Levain.

Sour Levain

3½ cups of Sourdough Starter

1 cup water

2¾ cups unbleached, organic flour

1⅛ teaspoons salt

— MAKES APPROXIMATELY 36 CUPS (15 POUNDS)

Put all the ingredients in a large bowl. Using a heavy-duty mixer fitted with a dough hook, knead for 8 minutes. Or, knead by hand on a lightly floured surface for 20-30 minutes. Place the dough in a plastic bag and seal. Refrigerate for at least 2 to 3 days to allow to ferment, but do not store it in this manner for more than 3 weeks.

Basic French Bread

2 cups cold water

7 ½ cups unbleached organic flour

2 teaspoons salt

1 cake fresh yeast (6 oz)

4 ½ to 5 cups (3 pounds) Sour Levain (see page 189)

1 egg, beaten, or olive oil, for brushing the loaves

—MAKES 4 LOAVES

Place all of the ingredients in a large mixing bowl. Using a heavy-duty mixer fitted with a dough hook, knead for 10 minutes. Or, knead by hand on a lightly floured board for 20-30 minutes. Place the dough in a plastic bag and seal. Place the bag in a bowl at room temperature until it has doubled in size.

Punch the dough down. Let the dough rise until it has doubled again. Punch the dough down again.

Place a sheet pan on the lower rack of the oven, and preheat the oven to 425°. Remove the dough from the plastic bag and cut it into 4 pieces. Shape the dough into round or long tapered loaves.

Dust 2 baking sheets with cornmeal. Place 2 loaves on each pan and cover loosely with plastic wrap. Let sit at room temperature until doubled.

Brush the loaves with the beaten egg or olive oil. Place the pans on the top rack and pour 1 cup cold water into the sheet pan on the lower rack. Close the oven door immediately. (This creates steam, which seals the outside of the loaf and helps produce a fine crust.) Bake for 35 to 45 minutes, or until golden brown.

Gold Medal Winner for Cold Bread Specialties

Prepare the Basic French Bread dough through the second rise. Punch the dough down and place it in a large bowl. Mix in the following ingredients at low speed until blended (not more than 60 seconds), or mix in by hand: 12 ounces hydrated sun-dried tomatoes (or 6 ounces dried); 12 ounces black olives; 6 Spanish Roja garlic cloves, chopped; and 8 ounces chopped French Red shallots. Proceed with recipe as directed.

Silver Medal Winner for Cold Bread Specialties

Prepare the Basic French Bread dough through the second rise. Punch the dough down and place it in a large bowl. Mix in the following ingredients at low speed until blended (not more than 60 seconds), or mix in by hand: 8 Purple Tip garlic cloves, roasted (see page 179); 1 red onion, chopped; frozen spinach, thawed, squeezed dry, and chopped; 1 cup (4 ounces) grated Gouda cheese; 1 cup (4 ounces) grated Muenster cheese. Proceed with recipe as directed.

Gold Medal Winner for Hot Bread Specialties

Prepare the Basic French Bread dough through the second rise. Punch the dough down and place it in a large bowl. Mix in the following ingredients at low speed until blended (not more than 60 seconds), or mix in by hand: 3 cups (16 ounces) grated Jarlsberg cheese, and 3 cups (16 ounces) grated Sonoma County jack or Muenster cheese. Form the dough into balls and connect them to each other on baking sheets by pressing them together.

Variation: along with the cheese, add 10 minced Mexican garlic cloves and 10 minced fresh jalapeños.

Caution: don't add more than 3 cups of total ingredients into each batch of dough.

MAIN DISHES

Chester's Russian Spring Garlic Kasha

1 cup buckwheat groats (kasha)

1¾ cups water

1 cup garlic buds, from scapes, or ¾ cup minced garlic

2 large ripe tomatoes, finely chopped

2 cups fresh flat-leaf parsley sprigs, minced

1 cup minced fresh mint

¼ cup extra virgin olive oil

¾ cup fresh lime juice, or ¼ cup fresh lemon juice

2½ cups boiling chicken stock

— SERVES 6

Pour the groats into a medium bowl and add the water. Soak until all the water is absorbed (about 1 hour). Stir to fluff and separate the grains. Add the remaining ingredients. Taste, and adjust the seasonings with citrus juice, salt, and pepper, if desired.

Chester's Oakland-Famous Chicken-Kelly Paloma

1 tablespoon ground cumin

1 small poblano chile, seeded

1/4 cup fresh lemon juice, or 1/2 cup fresh lime juice

15 Shatili or Chesnok Red garlic cloves, squeezed through a garlic press

1 or 2 bay leaves

3 tablespoons extra virgin olive oil

One 4-pound chicken, cut into serving pieces and skinned

1/4 cup Calvado or applejack

1/2 cup water

1 bunch flat-leaf parsley or chopped green onion tops, for garnish

— Serves 6

Combine the cumin, chile, lemon or lime juice, garlic, bay leaf, and 1 tablespoon of the oil in a bowl large enough to hold the chicken. Add the chicken and marinate for 25 minutes.

Heat the remaining oil in a large skillet over medium heat and brown the chicken, not turning too often. Add the marinade, Calvados or applejack, and water. Cover and simmer for 20 minutes.

Transfer the pieces to a platter. Boil the sauce for 12 minutes, then pour it over the chicken. Garnish with parsley or onion greens.

Chester's Favorite Roasted Garlic-Pistachio Pasta

2 heads Duganskij (Czech) garlic

½ cup extra virgin olive oil

¼ cup chicken or beef stock

1 cup unsalted pistachios

Angel hair pasta

1 tablespoon minced fresh flat-leaf parsley

Salt and pepper to taste

— SERVES 2

Preheat the oven to 350°F.

Remove the outer skin from 1 head of garlic. Place the garlic head in a small baking dish and dribble ⅛ teaspoon of the oil over the garlic. Bake for 1 hour.

Add the stock and bake for 5 minutes. Let cool. Spread the pistachios on a baking sheet. Toast in the oven, stirring twice, for 5 minutes. Grind coarsely in a blender or food processor ¼ cup of the pistachios and set aside.

Peel and purée the cloves from the remaining head of garlic. In a small skillet, heat the purée in the remaining oil. Add the ground pistachios. Simmer over low heat for 5 minutes. Add the squeezed roasted cloves from the first garlic head, along with the remaining ¾ cup of the toasted pistachios, the parsley, salt and pepper. Stir well.

In a large pot of salted boiling water, cook the pasta until al dente. Drain. Add to the sauce in the skillet, toss, and serve immediately.

If-You-Dare Calamari

5 pounds calamari, cleaned and sliced

½ cup extra virgin olive oil

½ cup dry sherry

1 tablespoon minced fresh basil

Juice of 1 lemon

1 tablespoon minced fresh oregano

1 teaspoon red pepper flakes

¼ cup crushed Brown Tempest or Siberian garlic

½ cup dry white wine

— SERVES 4

Add the calamari and the olive oil to a heavy skillet. Cook over low heat for 20 minutes, stirring frequently. Add the sherry and let cook for 10 minutes. Add the basil, lemon juice, oregano, red pepper, and crushed garlic. Add the white wine. Cover and simmer for 10 minutes.

Tuna and Green Salad

Four 6-ounce cans solid tuna

1 head fresh escarole, chopped

1 head fresh romaine, chopped

10 tablespoons extra virgin olive oil

4 French Messadrone garlic cloves, minced

Salt and pepper to taste

— SERVES 6

Cut the tuna into small pieces, and set aside. Toss the next four ingredients together, then add the tuna. Mix gently, and season to taste with salt and pepper. Serve chilled.

Pasta Aglio e Olio

2 pounds dried pasta

2 heads Lorz Italian or Early Red Italian or California Early (yes, Gilroy!) or Russian Red Toch

1 cup extra virgin olive oil

1 teaspoon red pepper flakes

1 teaspoon salt

Juice of 1 lemon

A very large handful of flat-leaf parsley, chopped

— SERVES 6

In a large pot of salted boiling water, cook the pasta until al dente.

While the pasta cooks, prepare the sauce. In a medium skillet, saute the garlic in oil over low heat until the garlic is translucent, about 3 minutes. Add the red pepper flakes and salt. Add the lemon juice. Turn off heat.

When the oil is cool, add the parsley. Pour the hot drained pasta into a shallow serving bowl. Cover with the warm sauce. Mix well. Serve immediately.

Stuffed Tomatoes

6 large firm ripe tomatoes

Salt for sprinkling, plus salt to taste

2 tablespoons butter

2 tablespoons olive oil

8 ounces porcini or portobello or field mushrooms, finely chopped

Juice of ½ lemon

Salt and pepper, to taste

Pinch of ground chile pepper

3 Mexican garlic cloves, minced

Juice of ½ lime

2 tablespoons tomato paste

2 egg yolks, lightly beaten

1 teaspoon chopped fresh cilantro or basil

Butter at room temperature for spreading

6 bread slices, cut to fit on top of tomatoes

— Serves 6

Preheat the oven to 350°F.

Cut off the tops of the tomatoes, core, and remove seeds. Sprinkle the insides of the tomatoes with salt and invert on a rack to drain.

In a large skillet over medium heat, melt the butter with the oil. Add the mushrooms and cook for 10 minutes.

Add the lemon juice, salt and pepper to taste, chile pepper, garlic, and lime juice. Cook for 6 to 8 minutes, or until the juices are almost evaporated.

Blend the tomato paste and egg yolks together and stir into the mushrooms. Stir in the cilantro or basil. Stuff the tomatoes with the mushroom mixture. Butter the bread slices. Top each tomato with 1 bread slice. Bake for 10 to 15 minutes or until the bread is brown.

Pasta con Spirito

½ cup plus 1 tablespoon extra virgin olive oil

2 bunches fresh basil, stemmed and shredded

15 Roma tomatoes, quartered

8 Purple Tip garlic cloves, minced

½ teaspoon salt

¼ teaspoon pepper

1 pound angel hair pasta

Grated cheese of your choice

— Serves 6 to 8

Pour the ½ cup oil into a large bowl. Add the basil, tomatoes, garlic, ¼ teaspoon of the salt, and the pepper to the oil. Let sit at room temperature for 2 to 3 hours, stirring occasionally.

Ten minutes before serving, bring a large pot of water to a boil. Meanwhile, pour the basil mixture into a large skillet and place over low heat. Add the remaining ¼ teaspoon of salt to the boiling water. Add the pasta and cook until al dente. Drain.

Place the pasta in a large bowl. Add the remaining 1 tablespoon of oil and toss. Add the warm basil mixture. Serve immediately, topped with cheese.

Quick, Simple, and Elegant Pasta

1 pound linguine

4 ounces salted whole cashews or walnut halves

½ cup plus 1 tablespoon extra virgin olive oil

¼ teaspoon salt

¼ teaspoon pepper

6 Rose du Var garlic cloves, minced

8 to 10 basil leaves or flat-leaf parsley, shredded

Grated, hard cheese of your choice

—Serves 6 to 8

In a large pot of salted boiling water, cook the linguine until al dente. While the pasta cooks, add the nuts, ½ cup of the oil, salt, pepper, and garlic to a small skillet. Warm over low heat.

Drain the linguine and place it in a large bowl. Add the 1 tablespoon of oil and toss. Add the nut mixture and toss. Top with basil or parsley and pass the cheese at the table.

Melanzane Deliciose

2 large firm eggplants (1 to 2 pounds each), halved lengthwise

½ cup extra virgin olive oil

1 pound lean meat of choice, cut into small cubes

8 large ripe tomatoes, peeled and chopped

Salt and black pepper to taste

1 cup dry white wine

8 Medidzhvari garlic cloves, minced

1 cup dried bread crumbs

1 cup chopped flat-leaf parsley

¼ cup grated cheese of choice

Whole fresh basil leaves or flat-leaf parsley, for garnish

—Serves 4 to 6

Spoon the pulp out of the eggplants, leaving a 1-inch-thick shell. Reserve the pulp in a bowl. Steam the eggplant halves until just tender; set aside.

In a medium skillet over medium heat, heat the oil and sauté the meat until browned. Stir in the eggplant pulp, tomatoes, salt, pepper, and wine. Cook for 10 minutes. Add the garlic and cook for 5 minutes. In a small bowl, mix the bread crumbs, parsley, and grated cheese. Place the eggplant shells in a baking pan. Fill the shells with the eggplant pulp mixture and top with the bread crumb mixture.

Bake, uncovered, for 30 minutes, or until the crumbs are brown. Garnish with basil or parsley and serve.

Picnic Circolo

1 large round, high-domed French or Italian bread loaf

2 eggs

1 cup milk

6 chicken legs

6 chicken breasts

3 cups bread crumbs

⅓ cup light vegetable oil

⅔ cup extra virgin olive oil

1/2 teaspoon salt

Pinch of red pepper flakes

1½ teaspoons poultry seasoning

8 Metechi garlic cloves, roasted (see page 179)

3 sprigs fresh rosemary

—Serves 6 to 8

Preheat the oven to 375°F.

Cut off the top of the bread and set aside. Pull the soft bread out of the loaf, leaving a wall 1 inch thick. Cut the soft bread into ¾-inch-thick cubes and set aside. Place the bread shell in the oven to warm. In a shallow bowl, mix the eggs and milk together. Dry the chicken pieces on paper towels. Dip each piece into the egg mixture and then into the bread crumbs.

Heat the vegetable oil in a large skillet over medium-high heat. Add the chicken pieces and brown. Using tongs, transfer the chicken to a plate. Reserve the pan and the drippings. Add ⅓ cup of the olive oil, the salt, pepper flakes, and poultry seasoning to the skillet and heat. Add the cubed bread and brown lightly over medium head. Set aside.

In a small bowl, combine the roasted garlic, rosemary, and remaining ⅓ cup olive oil. With a rubber spatula, coat the inside of the warmed bread and the underside of the bread lid with the garlic mixture. Fill the bread cavity with the chicken and cubed bread. Place the lid in place as tightly as possible. Bake for 1 hour. Serve the loaf at the table. Remove the lid and the rosemary. Guests can spoon out the filling and cut pieces of crust as desired.

Chicken Paprikash

10 ounces dried wild mushrooms

½ cup all-purpose flour

⅛ teaspoon ground nutmeg

2 teaspoons hot paprika

½ teaspoon black pepper

½ cup olive oil

6 chicken legs

6 chicken breasts

½ cup dry sherry

¼ cup chicken stock or canned low-salt broth

6 Purple Tip garlic cloves, minced

1 onion, chopped

2 cups sour cream at room temperature

— Serves 6 to 8

Soak the dried mushrooms in boiling water for 15 minutes.

Drain and dry between paper towels.

In a shallow bowl, combine the flour, nutmeg, paprika, and pepper. Coat the chicken pieces in this mixture. In a heavy, large skillet over medium heat, heat the oil and brown the chicken. Combine the sherry and stock and pour over the chicken. Cut any large mushrooms into pieces and add to the skillet. Cover the skillet and simmer until tender (about 45 minutes).

Add the garlic cloves and onion to the sour cream, blend, and pour over the chicken.

Potato Garlic Fritatta

½ cup (1 stick) plus 1 tablespoon unsalted butter

1 large Bermuda onion, coarsely chopped

Salt and pepper to taste

5 pounds Yukon Gold potatoes, cut into ½-inch cubes

6 Creole Red garlic cloves

½ cup vegetable oil

10 green onions, chopped

1 pound mushrooms

2 red bell peppers, seeded, deveined, and chopped

1 dozen eggs

4 cups (1 pound) grated cheese of choice

¾ cup Italian bread crumbs

1 tablespoon dried oregano

1 tablespoon dried rosemary

½ tablespoon dried lemon sage

2 tablespoons freshly ground pepper

2 teaspoons salt

Hot paprika for sprinkling

— SERVES 20 AS AN APPETIZER OR 8 TO 10 AS A MAIN COURSE

In a large skillet over medium heat, melt the ½ cup butter. Add the onion, salt, and pepper and sauté for 10 minutes. Add the potatoes. cover and cook for 15 minutes, stirring occasionally. Add the garlic. Uncover and cook, stirring occasionally, until the potatoes are brown and tender, about 30 to 45 minutes, adding the vegetable oil as necessary. Set aside.

Preheat the oven to 375°F. In a large skillet over medium heat, heat the 1 tablespoon butter and green onions until tender. Add the mushrooms and sauté for 5 minutes. Add the red peppers and sauté for 3 minutes. Let cool.

In a large bowl, beat the eggs. Fold in the cheese, bread crumbs, herbs, pepper, and salt. Stir into the potato mixture. Pour into two 10-inch round cake pans. Sprinkle with paprika. Bake for 40 to 50 minutes, or until crust is brown.

Scallops in Garlic Sauce

2 tablespoons extra virgin olive oil

4 French Red shallots, sliced lengthwise

12 ounces (2⅓ cups) pine nuts

2 large portobello mushrooms, sliced

2 pounds scallops

7 Italian Red garlic cloves, roasted (see page 179)

3 tablespoons cornstarch mixed with 3 tablespoons water

2 teaspoons salt

¼ teaspoon white pepper

⅔ cup sliced green onions

— SERVES 5 TO 6

In a small skillet over medium heat, heat 1 tablespoon of the olive oil. Add the shallots, cover, and cook for 3 minutes. Add the pine nuts, cover, and cook for 3 minutes. Add the mushrooms, cover and cook for 3 minutes. Set aside.

Add 3 quarts water to a large saucepan and add the scallops. Bring to a boil, then drain immediately and rinse the scallops in cold water. Drain again.

In a wok over medium-high heat, heat the remaining 1 tablespoon oil. Add the garlic and stir-fry for 1 minute. Stir in the cornstarch mixture, salt, and pepper. Stir in the shallot mixture. Add the scallops and cook, stirring gently, until the sauce thickens and coats the scallops, 3 to 4 minutes.

Sprinkle with the green onions and serve.

Local Color's Cornish Hens

This recipe and the one on page 207 are from the Local Color Cafe *in Occidental, California.*

10 Asian Tempest garlic cloves, minced

½ cup olive oil

Salt and pepper to taste

2 Cornish hens

6 rosemary sprigs

6 thyme sprigs

6 oregano sprigs

½ cup homemade chicken stock or canned low-fat broth

— SERVES 2

Preheat oven to 375°F.

In a small bowl, combine the garlic, oil, salt, and pepper. Rub the oil mixture on the inside and outside of both hens. Stuff the hens with half the fresh herbs. Lay the remaining herbs on top of hens.

Bake the hens, basting them with the stock or broth every 15 minutes, for 45 minutes, or until hens are golden brown.

Polenta from the Sea

6 ounces dried porcini mushrooms

½ cup extra virgin olive oil

6 rosemary sprigs

4 Creole Red garlic heads, roasted (see page 179)

2 red bell peppers, seeded, deveined, and cut into thin strips

½ teaspoon Dijon mustard

3 tablespoons chopped fresh oregano

1¼ teaspoon salt, plus salt to taste

Pepper to taste

10 cups water

3 large portobello mushrooms, sliced

1 cup chopped flat-leaf parsley

1 10- to 12-ounce salmon fillet

1 10- to 12-ounce Red Snapper fillet

3 cups polenta

3 tablespoons unsalted butter

½ cup (2 ounces) grated cheese of choice

— SERVES 6

Soak the porcini mushrooms in boiling water to cover for 1 hour. In a small skillet over very low heat, heat all but ¼ teaspoon of the olive oil, add the rosemary sprigs, and steep for 10 minutes. Remove and discard the rosemary. Add the roasted garlic and pepper strips and stir-fry for 5 minutes. Stir in the mustard, oregano, and salt and pepper to taste.

Meanwhile, in a double boiler, bring the water to a boil. Add the 1 ¼ teaspoon salt to the water.

In a large skillet over high heat, heat the remaining ¼ teaspoon of the olive oil. Add the salmon and snapper fillets and cook for 3 minutes on each side. Transfer to a cutting board and cut each fillet into bite-sized pieces. Set aside.

When the water is boiling, gradually stir in the polenta. Continue to stir until the polenta is thickened and not grainy, about 25 minutes. Stir in the butter. Stir in the fish pieces.

Spoon half of the polenta onto a serving platter. Sprinkle ¼ cup of the cheese on the polenta. Add the remaining polenta. Pour the garlic mixture over the polenta. Sprinkle the remaining ¼ cup grated cheese on top and serve.

Local Color's Apricot Chicken

3½ pounds of chicken, cut into serving pieces

Salt and pepper to taste

6 Inchelium Red garlic cloves, minced

6 fresh thyme sprigs

Juice of 3 lemons

1 cup apricot preserves

—Serves 2 to 4

Preheat the oven to 350°F.

Rub the chicken pieces with salt, pepper, and garlic. Place the chicken in one layer in a baking dish. Lay the fresh thyme sprigs over the chicken. Stir lemon juice and apricot preserves together and pour over the chicken pieces.

Bake for 50 minutes or until golden brown.

Stir-fried Vegetables with Garlic and Peanut Butter

1 carrot, cut into rounds

1 cup pine nuts

3 tablespoons olive oil

¾ pound large French Red shallots, sliced

1 7-ounce can whole green chiles (mild)

3 tablespoons peanut butter of choice

1 8-ounce can water chestnuts, drained and sliced

1 each green and red bell peppers, seeded, deveined, and cut into strips

8 Inchelium Red garlic cloves, roasted (see page 179)

1 zucchini, cut into rounds

2 yellow crookneck squashes, cut into rounds

2 tablespoons soy sauce

Salt and pepper to taste

— Serves 6 to 8

In a medium saucepan of boiling water, cook the carrots for 6 minutes. Drain and set aside.

In a wok over low heat, stir-fry the pine nuts in the oil for 4 minutes. Add the shallots and cook 4 minutes.

Add the chiles, peanut butter, water chestnuts, bell peppers, and garlic. Increase heat to medium and cook for 5 minutes. Add the carrots, zucchini, and squashes. Cook for 5 minutes

Add the soy sauce and cook 4 minutes.

TWO GARLICKY DESSERTS

Poached Hosui Pears

1 bottle Burgundy wine

¾ cup kirsch or Benedictine liqueur

2 cups sugar

1 bay leaf

2 unpeeled Inchelium Red garlic heads

Julienned zest of 1 orange and 1 lemon

8 Hosui pears, cored, peeled and left whole

½ cup raspberry or boysenberry preserves, or whole cranberry sauce

2 cups raspberry, boysenberries, or cranberries

Bring the wine, kirsch or Benedictine, and sugar to a boil. Add the bay leaf, whole heads of garlic, and lemon and orange zest. Cook for 8 minutes over low heat for 5 minutes.

Reduce heat and let simmer. Add the pears and cook for 5 minutes, gently turning over at 2½ minutes.

Using a slotted spoon, remove the pears and let cool. Cook the syrup over low heat to reduce to 2 cups. Strain through a fine-meshed sieve. Add the preserves and berries. Simmer for 1 minute.

Pour the warm mixture over the cool pears. Let cool. Serve.

Caroline Salz's Upside-Down Hosui Cake

½ cup butter, melted

¼ cup brown sugar

8 to 10 thick slices Hosui pears

1 cup honey

8 to 12 Inchelium Red garlic cloves

1 pound cake mix of choice

— SERVES 8 TO 10

Preheat the oven to 350°F.

Spread the butter on the bottom of an 8 x 10 baking dish. Sprinkle with the brown sugar. Arrange one layer of pears over the honey. In the center of each slice place 1 garlic clove.

Mix the cake batter and pour into the prepared pan. Bake for 30 to 35 minutes.

Let cool for 10 to 15 minutes on a rack. Slip a knife around edges to loosen from the pan. Unmold on a serving plate. Serve at room temperature.

RESOURCES:

biosys
10150 Old Columbia Road
Columbia, Maryland 21046
(410) 381-3800
Biological pesticides and insecticides based on environmentally safe and naturally occurring agents such as nematodes.

Filaree Farm—Filaree Productions.
Rt. 2, Box 162
Okanogan, Washington 98840
(509) 422-6940
Locally grown, organic garlic seed. Limited supply.

Seed Savers Exchange
3076 North Winn Rd.
Decorah, Iowa 52101
(319) 382-5990
Seed and planting instructions for vegetables, flowers, and tobacco from U.S., Russian, and Polish sources.

SUGGESTED READING:

Kourik, Robert. *Designing and Maintaining Your Edible Landscape Naturally.* Santa Rosa, CA.: Metamorphic Press, 1986.

———. *Drip Irrigation For Every Landscape and All Climates* Santa Rosa, CA.: Metamorphic Press, 1992.

———. *Gray Water Use in the Landscape*. Santa Rosa, CA.: Metamorphic Press, 1988.

Manweiler, Stephen and Dr. Ramon Georgis. "Entomopathogenic Nematodes: A Developing Biological Control Technology." *Agricultural Zoology Reviews* 6 (October 1994): 63-94.

More books from Ten Speed Press

Garlic Lovers' Greatest Hits
Fifteen years of prize-winning recipes
by the Gilroy Garlic Festival
Each July, the town of Gilroy, California hosts a gourmet extravaganza: a garlic festival that has captured international acclaim. Here are 150 of the best-loved recipes from the last 15 years. 128 pages.

The Complete Garlic Lovers' Cookbook
by the Gilroy Garlic Festival
Features garlic-infused recipes from around the world, including France, the Philippine Islands, Portugal, China, Greece, and India. Also includes a garlic glossary, garlic history, and good things to know about garlic! 376 pages.

The Pepper Garden
by Dave DeWitt & Paul Bosland
Everything you need to know to grow exotic chile peppers in your backyard: step-by-step instructions, a list of seed sources, a glossary of terms, recipes, harvesting techniques, and drying and roasting tips. 256 pages.

The Habanero Cookbook
by Dave DeWitt & Nancy Gerlach
Filled with color photos, it shows the reader the full picture of the world's hottest chile pepper—how it is grown, how it is used, and how to make it a very exciting addition to a culinary scene. Over 100 recipes are included. 176 pages.

Totally Garlic Cookbook
by Helene Siegel & Karen Gillingham

> This is a buy you can't beat...Wonderfully inventive recipes —easy to make, very flavorful, and innovatively original, rather than a mere rehash.
>
> —*World of Cookbooks*

This die-cut little book is perfect for anyone who can't get enough of their favorite herb. Its unusual recipes include garlic tea, garlic brandy, and garlic crème caramel. 96 pages.

For more information, or to order, call the publisher at the number below. We accept VISA, Mastercard, and American Express. You may also wish to write for our free catalog of over 500 books, posters, and audiotapes.

Ten Speed Press • P.O. Box 7123 • Berkeley, CA 94710
(800) 841-BOOK • Fax (510) 524-1052